BALLARD HIGH SCHOOL LIBRARY

Student Handbook to Psychology

Brain and Mind

Volume III

Student Handbook to Psychology

Brain and Mind

Volume III

MICHAEL KERCHNER

Bernard C. Beins
General Editor

An Infobase Learning Company

Student Handbook to Psychology: Brain and Mind
Copyright © 2012 Michael Kerchner

Facts On File, Inc.
An Imprint of Infobase Learning
132 West 31st Street
New York NY 10001

Library of Congress Cataloging-in-Publication Data
Student handbook to psychology / [edited by] Bernard C. Beins.
    v. ; cm.
  Includes bibliographical references and index.
  Contents: v. 1. History, perspectives, and applications / Kenneth D. Keith—v. 2. Methods and measurements / Bernard C. Beins—v. 3. Brain and mind / Michael Kerchner—v. 4. Learning and thinking / Christopher M. Hakala and Bernard C. Beins—v. 5. Developmental psychology / Lynn Shelley—v. 6. Personality and abnormal psychology / Janet F. Carlson—v. 7. Social psychology / Jeffrey D. Holmes and Sheila K. Singh.
  ISBN 978-0-8160-8280-3 (set : alk. paper)—ISBN 978-0-8160-8281-0 (v. 1 : alk. paper)—ISBN 978-0-8160-8286-5 (v. 2 : alk. paper)—ISBN 978-0-8160-8285-8 (v. 3 : alk. paper)—ISBN 978-0-8160-8284-1 (v. 4 : alk. paper)—ISBN 978-0-8160-8282-7 (v. 5 : alk. paper)—ISBN 978-0-8160-8287-2 (v. 6 : alk. paper)—ISBN 978-0-8160-8283-4 (v. 7 : alk. paper) 1. Psychology—Textbooks.
I. Beins, Bernard.
  BF121.S884 2012
  150—dc23   2011045277

Text design by Erika K. Arroyo
Cover design by Takeshi Takahashi
Composition by EJB Publishing Services
Cover printed by Yurchak Printing, Landisville, Pa.
Book printed and bound by Yurchak Printing, Landisville, Pa.
Date printed: September 2012
Printed in the United States of America

CONTENTS

PREFACE

Behavior is endlessly fascinating. People and other animals are complicated creatures that show extraordinary patterns of abilities, intelligence, social interaction, and creativity along with, unfortunately, problematic behaviors. All of these characteristics emerge because of the way the brain interprets incoming information and directs our responses to that information.

This seven-volume **Student Handbook to Psychology** set highlights important and interesting facets of thought and behavior. It provides a solid foundation for learning about psychological processes associated with growth and development, social issues, thinking and problem solving, and abnormal thought and behavior. Most of the major schools and theories related to psychology appear in the books in the series, albeit in abbreviated form. Because psychology is such a highly complex and diverse discipline, these volumes present a broad overview of the subject rather than a complete and definitive treatise. Such a work, in fact, would be difficult (if not impossible) because psychological scientists are still searching for answers to a great number of questions. If you are interested in delving in more depth into specific areas of psychology, we have provided a bibliography of accessible readings to help you fill in the details.

The volumes in this series follow the order that you might see in a standard presentation on a variety of topics, but each book stands alone and the series does not need to be read in any particular order. In fact, you can peruse individual chapters in each volume at will, seeking out and focusing on those topics that interest you most. On the other hand, if you do choose to read through a complete volume, you will find a flow of information that connects related sections of the books, providing a coherent overview of the entire discipline of psychology.

The authors of the seven volumes in this series are experts in their respective fields, so you will find psychological concepts that are up to date and that reflect the most recent advances in scientific knowledge about thought and behavior. In addition, each of the authors is an excellent writer who has presented the information in an interesting and compelling fashion. Although some of the material and many of the ideas are complex, the authors have done an outstanding job of conveying those ideas in ways that are both interesting and effective.

In *History, Perspectives, and Applications*, Professor Kenneth Keith of the University of San Diego has woven historical details into a tapestry that shows how psychological questions originated within a philosophical framework, incorporated biological concepts, and ultimately evolved into a single scientific discipline that remains interconnected with many other academic and scientific disciplines. Dr. Keith has identified the major figures associated with the development of the field of psychology as well as the social forces that helped shape their ideas.

In *Methods and Measurements*, I illustrate how psychologists create new knowledge through research. The volume presents the major approaches to research and explains how psychologists develop approaches to research that help us answer questions about complex aspects of behavior. Without these well-structured and proven research methods, we would not have much of the information we now have about behavior. Furthermore, these methods, approaches, and practices provide confidence that the knowledge we do have is good knowledge, grounded in solid research.

Many people are under the impression that each thought or behavior is a single thing. In *Brain and Mind*, Professor Michael Kerchner of Washington College dispels this impression by showing how the myriad structures and functions of our brain work in unison to create those seemingly simple and one-dimensional behaviors. As the author explains, each behavior is really the result of many different parts of the brain engaging in effective communication with one another. Professor Kerchner also explains what occurs when this integration breaks down.

Learning and Thinking, co-authored by Professor Christopher Hakala of Western New England College and me (at Ithaca College), explores the fascinating field of cognitive psychology, a discipline focused on the processes by which people learn, solve problems, and display intelligence. Cognitive psychology is a fascinating field that explores how we absorb information, integrate it, and then act on it.

In *Developmental Psychology*, Professor Lynn Shelley of Westfield State University addresses the very broad area of psychology that examines how people develop and change from the moment of conception through old age. Dr. Shelley's detailed and compelling explanation includes a focus on how maturation and environment play a part in shaping how each individual grows, evolves, and changes.

In *Personality and Abnormal Psychology*, Professor Janet Carlson of the Buros Center for Testing at the University of Nebraska (Lincoln) addresses various dimensions of personality, highlighting processes that influence normal and abnormal facets of personality. Dr. Carlson also explains how psychologists study the fundamental nature of personality and how it unfolds.

The final volume in this series is *Social Psychology*. Co-authored by Professor Jeffrey Holmes of Ithaca College and Sheila Singh of Cornell University, this volume examines how our thoughts and behaviors emerge in connection with our interactions with other people. As the authors of this volume explain, changes in a person's social environment can lead to notable changes in the way that person thinks and behaves.

As editor of this series, I have had the opportunity to work with all of the authors who have contributed their expertise and insights to this project. During this collaborative process, I found that we have much in common. All of us have spent our careers pondering why people think and act the way they do. For every answer we come up with, we also develop new questions that are just as interesting and important. And we all agree that you cannot find a more interesting subject to study than psychology.

As you learn about psychology, we hope that the information in these seven volumes inspires the same fascination in you. We also hope that our explanations, illustrations, and narrative studies motivate you to continue studying why we humans are the way we are.

—Bernard C. Beins, Ph.D., Professor of Psychology,
Ithaca College, Series Editor

CHAPTER 1

PHYSIOLOGICAL METHODS OF STUDYING BEHAVIOR

Imagine your family lived with the recognition that a certain number of your relations in each generation before had been afflicted with a baffling and devastating disorder characterized by bizarre behaviors, troubling auditory hallucinations and disturbing and irrational thoughts. How might you begin to search for an explanation and possibly a cure? Or at least determine how these symptoms might be diminished to the point that some semblance of normality might be restored and the quality of life improved for those so afflicted? What possible explanations would you entertain? How would you test each of these explanations?

Perhaps you might begin to collect as much information as you could about the individuals in your family and those in other families who had been victims of this devastating disorder. You might carefully collect individual histories regarding those relatives who are now diseased, and make detailed observations of living relatives who do and do not have the disorder. Specifically, you may look for commonalities among those individuals who are afflicted with the disorder and for features that distinguish them from unaffected individuals. By compiling and comparing, detailed case histories of these individuals patterns would emerge that would help you narrow down the disorder's possible causes and provide clues that would allow you to generate hypotheses and guide you in the search for the cure you desire.

It is instructive to recognize that your initial list of explanations would depend to a great extent on existing knowledge and beliefs regarding what

1

guides human behaviors, the culture in which you reside, and the period in time when you live. If you had lived in Greece during the 4th century BC, you would have likely attributed maladies to an imbalance among various bodily humors, including blood. The philosopher Aristotle believed that the brain functioned merely as a means to cool the blood, and that the soul that animated an

TABLE 1.1.
Some Examples of Neurological and Psychiatric Case Studies That Have Helped Advance Understanding of Brain Function

Memory	
"H.M." Henry Molaison	Episodic memory deficits resulting from bilateral resection of the hippocampus and surrounding neural structures.
"K.C."	A second case of anterograde episodic amnesia similar to H.M., resulting from bilateral damage to the hippocampus caused by traumatic brain injury.
Clive Wearing	Episodic memory deficits resulting from bilateral degeneration of the hippocampus caused by encephalitis.
"A.J." Jill Price	*Hyperthymesia:* Exceptional autobiographical memory; only three contemporary cases of hyperthymesia have been confirmed. In all cases this appears to be a congenital/developmental ability.
Language	
Laborgne ("Tan") & Lelong	Profound deficits in speech production resulting from damage to Broca's area, a region in the frontal lobe of the brain's left hemisphere.
Victor Aveyron	The Wild Child of Aveyron: a "feral child" presumed to have matured in isolation in the woods, in the absence of exposure to spoken language, with resulting impairments in language acquisition.
Genie	Extreme deficits in language acquisition resulting from early isolation, and parental abuse/neglect.
Howard Engel	*Alexia:* A profound impairment in the ability to perceive written passages —"Word Blindness". Engle is a writer who awoke one morning to find that he was unable to recognize words on a printed page. Nevertheless, he was able to write.

individual resided in the heart. It was not until many centuries later that evidence had accumulated to generate consensus that the brain, and not the heart, controlled our thoughts and actions. Case studies of individuals with various types of brain injuries contributed much of this evidence, and continue to guide neuroscientists in furthering our understanding of brain function.

Psychopathology	
The Genain Quadruplets	Nora, Iris, Myra, & Hester (NIMH). A set of identical quadruplet sisters, all of whom were diagnosed as schizophrenic.
Perception	
"L.M.," Gisela Leibold	*Akinetopsia; Movement Agnosia:* Gisela possesses normal visual acuity and can identify objects by sight; however, a stroke that has damaged the cortical region identified as V5, has deprived her of the ability to perceive objects as they move.
V.Q., W.K., F.A., and others	*Phantom Limb:* Following the traumatic and sudden loss of a limb, some patients still perceive that the limb is nonetheless attached, that it may move or be contorted in painful positions.
J.C.	*Alien Limb Syndrome:* A condition in which brain-damaged patients experience their limbs performing seemingly purposeful acts without their intention. The "alien" limb may interfere with the actions of their normal limb, leading to the misperception that its actions are directed by another entity.
D.L., C.N., and others	*Amusia:* Impairments in the perception of music resulting from stroke, tumor, neurodegenerative disease, or traumatic brain injury. In most cases, the impairments result from damage localized within the temporal lobes of the right hemisphere. There are also cases of congenital developmental amusia. Impairments in perception of rhythm, tone, or emotion may occur in musically trained or naïve individuals.
D.B., G.Y.	*Blindsight:* These individuals are blind as a result of damage to the occipital lobes of the brain. Although they say they cannot see, they may be able to detect movement, avoid objects in their path, or identify objects visually better than would be expected based upon chance.
Dr. P, O. Sacks, C. Close	*Prosopagnosia:* Although tests reveal these patients have normal visual acuity and can accurately identify objects, even describe the appearance of someone's facial features, they have difficulty identifying individual faces—in some cases even their own face in the mirror. The phenomenon is typically associated with bilateral damage to certain regions within the temporal lobes of the brain.

CASE HISTORY STUDIES OF BRAIN FUNCTION

Initially, much of what scientists discerned about both normal and abnormal functions of the brain was the result of detailed studies of individuals who either suffered some injury to the brain or who were experiencing an unusual neurological or psychological disability. Such case studies have played a significant role in our initial characterization and early investigations into the etiology and treatment of disorders such as Alzheimer disease, Parkinson disease, schizophrenia, autism, and language/speech disorders. You are likely to encounter some of these (see Table 1.1) in subsequent chapters of this book.

In the mid 1800s, for example, a French physician named Paul Broca reported on two individuals with distinctive impairments in their ability to speak. Their names were Laborgne and Lelong. Laborgne (a 51-year-old male) was able to produce only a single utterance ("Tan"), whereas Lelong (an 84-year-old male) had been able to utter just five words after having suffered a stroke. After each of these men had died, Broca was able to examine their brains and found that both men had damage to the frontal lobe on the left side of the brain in approximately the same location. This region of the brain is now known as Broca's area and appears, as Broca suggested, to serve an important role in the process of generating speech. Damage to this region with the resulting deficits in language production is known as Broca's Aphasia. Case studies have played similar roles in determining that other areas of the brain play important roles in our ability to comprehend speech. Using sophisticated neuroimaging technologies, modern researchers have obtained evidence that confirms the role that Broca's area has with regard to speech production and as well as other cognitive and motor processes besides speech.

Perhaps the most well known case study is that of Phineas Gage. In 1848, Gage was employed as a supervisor of a team of workmen who were laying tracks for a new section of railway outside the town of Cavendish, Vermont. An accidental detonation of an explosive charge launched a 3-foot 7-inch iron rod used to set the explosive charge into the air. Unfortunately, the rod entered Gage's head just below his left eye, damaging a significant portion of the frontal lobe as it exited through the top of his skull. It is unclear if Gage lost consciousness, but most remarkable is that he survived at all, and then recovered sufficiently to return home after 10 weeks. But, Gage's personality underwent a dramatic change. Whereas he had been relatively even tempered and contemplative, after the accident he became very ill tempered, impulsive, and inattentive. From this dramatic case, as well as others in which the frontal lobes have been damaged due to trauma or disease, psychologists and neurologists have recognized that the frontal lobes of the brain play important roles in many higher-order functions that contribute to the personal characteristics distinguishing each of us as individuals.

Cases such as those concerning Broca's patients and Gage result from acts of nature or chance; that is to say they are not cases that result from the intentional

Phineas Gage holding the tamping iron that passed through his skull and damaged his prefrontal cortex. *(Wikipedia)*

intervention of investigators. There are other instances, however, in which surgical interventions have been deemed ethically necessary although they necessitate the destruction of specific brain regions/structures. Because the surgeons involved precisely determine the damage, these cases differ from those in which damage is left to chance. Very often such cases present very unique insights regarding brain function.

One such instance is the case of Henry Molaison. To protect his privacy, Molaison's initials were all that identified him in the scientific literature prior to his death in 2008. As a young man, H.M. experienced numerous and unremitting epileptic seizures. The first seizures had occurred when he was just nine years old. By the age of 18, H.M.'s seizures had become unresponsive to medications available at the time and had increased in frequency and severity. As a desperate effort to provide him with any relief from seizures and the possibility of a relative degree of normalcy, surgeons elected to attempt a radical procedure that had previously been conducted only with experimental animals. Because H.M.'s seizures originated from tissue located in the temporal lobes at both sides of his brain, the plan was to surgically remove the diseased tissue, thereby eliminating the source of the seizures. Although this surgery had not been performed in humans before, healthy primates that had undergone similar procedures appeared to function without obvious impairments. The surgery was successful in that the frequency and severity of the seizures were reduced, although not eliminated, and the previously ineffective medications were now more effective at reducing the severity of the remaining seizure activity.

There was, however, an unanticipated and unintended adverse consequence of the experimental treatment. H.M. was left with a profound and pervasive form of memory impairment. Although memories for facts and events in his life prior to the surgery appeared to be relatively unaffected, H.M. no longer appeared to have the ability to form new memories for events (episodes) that occurred after the surgery. Subsequent studies determined that H.M. retained the ability to form some new memories, just not episodic memories. This deficit indicates either that there are other memory systems that do not rely on those regions surgically removed by H.M.'s surgeons, or that some regions of the brain not normally involved in generating episodic memories are capable of acquiring these abilities once regions that normally serve this role are no longer capable of doing so. After his death, H.M.'s brain was carefully preserved and donated to a team of researchers at the University of California in San Diego who have meticulously sectioned the brain into 2,401 thin slices that will enable them to digitally reconstruct the brain and precisely map the regions that appear to play such a critical role in the formation of new episodic memories.

The ability of some regions of the brain to acquire abilities that other regions may typically serve illustrates that the functional organization of the brain is not fixed, but is malleable. This characteristic is known as plasticity. Prior to the past few decades, the brain's ability to reorganize itself had been vastly underestimated. Perhaps the most dramatic and profound examples of such plasticity are those cases in which surgeons have removed one or the other hemispheres of the brain. Sometimes this procedure, known as **hemispherectomy,** is done to eliminate devastating epileptic seizures that originate from one side of the brain and then engulf the entire brain in a storm of uncontrollable activity. As we age, the brain's ability to rewire itself diminishes, so children are the primary candidates for hemispherectomy. Relatively minor damage to one hemisphere in an adult can manifest itself in significant motor and sensory losses on one side of the body or possibly alter speech. However, because the brain's potential for plasticity is greater during childhood, children who undergo a hemispherectomy are capable of significant recovery of functions normally localized in the hemisphere that was removed.

While the lessons learned from case studies of brain damaged or mentally ill individuals have provided significant contributions to our knowledge regarding the functional organization of the brain and the pathologies that are the cause of various biobehavioral brain disorders, the case study approach has significant scientific limitations. Many of the most interesting cases are by nature rare and unique; therefore, the knowledge obtained from studying them may not apply generally to all individuals. Broca's conclusions regarding the speech area that now bears his name were bolstered by the relatively rare and timely coincidence of encountering two individuals with similar symptoms and pathologies.

Case studies are also limited by their focus on individuals with either pathological or exceptional brain disabilities or abilities. The three cases above all involved invasive procedures or accidents; i.e., cases in which the brain is physically damaged either intentionally or unintentionally. The changes in behavior that are the consequence of such damage are inferred to be the result of the loss of function served by the damaged neural structures. (Note that it is also possible that changes may be attributable to a gain in function somewhere else in the brain.) Often the nature and extent of the invasive event are not fully known until the person being studied has died and his or her brain can be examined. Arguably, studying such cases may not help us gain a full and accurate understanding of how the normally healthy brain is functionally organized. What if your intent is to study either the structure or the function of a living, healthy or unperturbed brain? What if your goal is to understand changes in brain function that occur throughout an individual's lifetime? To accomplish these types of studies, investigators rely on various non-invasive means of correlating distinctive patterns of activity or changes in the anatomy of the brain with changes in behavior, thoughts, or emotions.

NON-INVASIVE MEASURES OF NEURAL ACTIVITY

Computer Aided Tomography (CAT or CT) scans rely on serial cross-sectional X-ray images of the brain that may be reassembled into three-dimensional structural representations of the brain. Magnetic Resonance Imaging (MRI) is also utilized to construct a static three-dimensional representation of brain structure, but MRI can provide more precise images than CT scans, without risks associated with exposure to radiation. CT and MRI scans are very useful if your intent is to compare changes in brain structure that may occur across time (e.g., following recovery from brain surgery or a closed head injury) or between healthy individuals and individuals who are diagnosed with a neurodevelopmental or neurodegenerative disorder. A relatively new means for structurally imaging the brain is **Diffusor Tensor Imaging (DTI)**. This technology is particularly well suited to studies of the major fiber tracts that connect various brain regions.

These methods provide very instructive images of brain structure, however, they are not capable of providing real-time measurements of brain activity. Other non-invasive technologies have been developed to fill this gap.

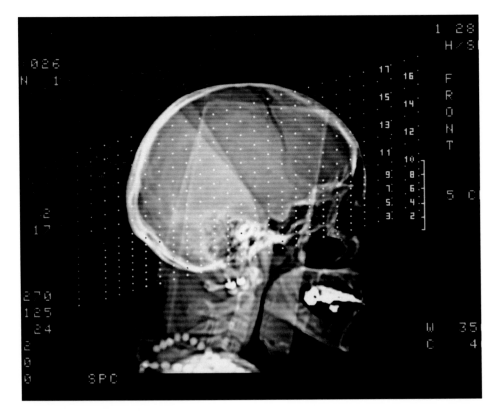

CAT scan of a woman's head. *(Shutterstock)*

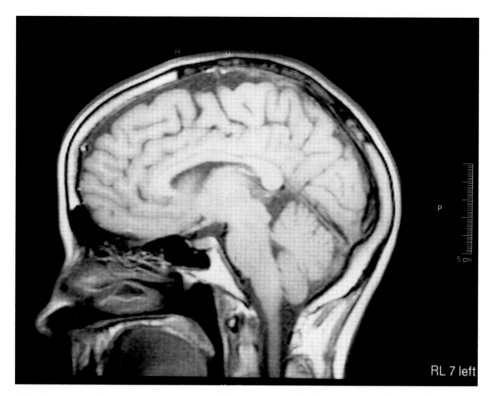

MRI scans use radio waves and powerful shifting magnetic fields to produce high-resolution images of healthy brain and diseased brain structures that are not as easily imaged using CAT. *(Shutterstock)*

Electroencephalography (EEG) employs numerous temporary surface electrodes that are applied to the scalp to record the sum of electrical activity generated by populations of brains cells within various regions of the brain. The millisecond temporal resolution of EEG is relatively fast, allowing precise correlations between rapid regional changes in neural activity and changes in sensory stimulation or cognitive demand. One measure of neural activity that is frequently employed in studies is a neuronal response pattern that is evoked by novel sensory stimuli. An example of such evoked potentials, or event related potentials (ERP) as they are also known, is shown in Figure 1.1. The large peak that occurs approximately 300 milliseconds after the stimulus is presented, is a prominent feature of the ERP, and aberrations in this neural response have been documented among individuals with a number of diverse neurocognitive and behavioral disorders, including schizophrenia, alcoholism, and posttraumatic stress disorder. These indications of aberrant patterns of ERP are consistent with symptoms of abnormal processing of sensory information in some component disorders.

Positron Emission Tomography (PET) is a non-invasive means of assessing regional neural activity based upon increases in blood flow in the most active regions of the brain via the accumulation of a radioisotope tracer molecule that is injected intravenously. PET scanners employ a ring of sensitive sensors to detect the emission of positrons from the tracers. By selectively choosing the tracers employed, specific biochemical processes with the brain can be localized

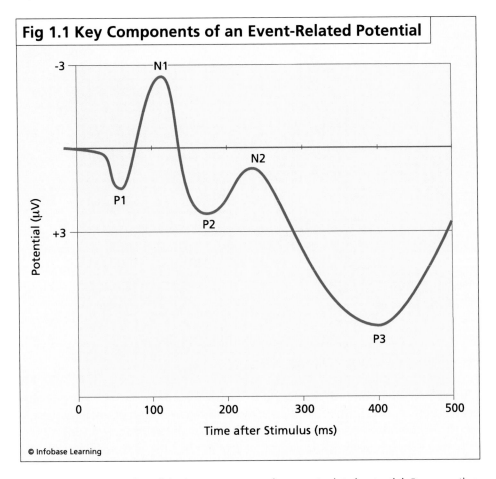

Fig 1.1 Key Components of an Event-Related Potential

A schematic representation of the key components of an event-related potential. By convention, negative changes from baseline are indicated by peaks and positive components of the ERP by troughs. The ERP is obtained by averaging neural responses over numerous presentation of a external sensory stimulus (i.e, an event). For example, a novel tone or visual stimulus, may occur unpredictably over the course of 100 trials, and the changes that occur in the EEG following these presentations is averaged to produce the ERP. The large P3 (P300) trough that occurs between 300 and 500 milliseconds after the event is commonly regarded as an indicator that such stimuli have been attended to and processed by the brain. Delays in the P3 response may be indicative of faulty processing.

and visualized. Although the temporal resolution of PET is not as great as that obtained by EEG, the advantage of PET is that it can be used to differentiate between various types of brain activity that EEG cannot; for example, activity that is dependent upon a specific chemical messenger such as the neurotransmitter dopamine. The function of dopamine and other neurotransmitters and neural regulators will be discussed in detail later in this chapter.

Like PET, **Single Photon Emission Computed Tomography (SPECT)** requires the administration of a radioisotope tracer. As this isotope decays, ultrasensitive detectors directly record the source of gamma emissions. Although the principle is similar to that which defines PET, the spatial resolution is not as good as is obtained using PET.

Whereas EEG, PET and SPECT are means of non-invasively monitoring regional changes in brain activity, when compared to functional Magnetic Resonance Imaging (fMRI), their abilities to accurately localize activity within small regions in the brain are limited. Like MRI, fMRI produces very detailed maps of brain structure with greater spatial resolution (2-3 mm) than EEG, while also providing temporal resolution comparable to that obtained by PET (several seconds to minutes). fMRI utilizes rapidly oscillating powerful magnetic fields to detect changes in oxygen utilization and demand in brain tissue and visually overlays this data on the anatomical MRI data. It is also possible to employ both EEG and fMRI simultaneously in order to combine the strengths of each in temporal and spatial resolution, respectively.

Magnetoencephalagrophy (MEG) uses highly sensitive detectors used to measure the very weak magnetic fields produced by the bioelectrical impulses the brain generates. Like EEG, it has very good temporal resolution but relatively poor spatial resolution and may be used in combination with MRI.

All neuroimaging techniques described above are non-invasive and non-manipulative; they are not intended to alter neural functioning, but merely to record what activity occurs. Therefore, by their nature, studies that employ these techniques are generally correlational. That is they may help identify distinctive patterns of brain activity that occur while someone is engaged in performing a cognitive or sensory task, but they cannot provide proof that such activation either causes the observed changes in cognitive or sensory performance, or is necessary for the task. To obtain evidence that may more conclusively establish that such activity causes the performance observed, a manipulative experimental study in which brain function is altered in a group of experimental participants and the outcome compared to measures obtained from an appropriate group of control participants is necessary. Would you volunteer to be a participant in the experimental group of such a study? Would you volunteer if there were a means of temporarily disrupting the normal function of a specific region of the brain, examining the outcome on thoughts, perceptions and behavior, then restoring brain function to normal without

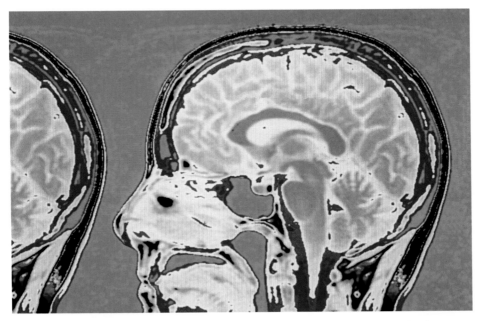

PET requires systemic injection of various tracer molecules that emit positrons under the influence of powerful radio frequency waves. The tracers accumulate in regions of the brain that are activated. *(Harry Sieplinga/HMS Images. Living Art Enterprises. Getty)*

apparent long-term adverse consequences? Recent technological advances have made this possible.

NON-INVASIVE EXPERIMENTAL MANIPULATION OF BRAIN FUNCTION

Just as the neural activity of the brain can create modest magnetic fields that can be recorded using MEG, non-invasive exposure to pulsating magnetic fields at the surface of the scalp can temporarily and reversibly disrupt neural activity. The technique used for this purpose is called **Transcranial Magnetic Stimulation (TMS)**. TMS directed over the region of the left hemisphere corresponding to Broca's area has been successfully employed to temporarily induce the same difficulties generating speech experienced by patients with Broca's Aphasia. Investigators have also begun to explore the feasibility of using repetitive TMS (rTMS) therapeutically. Several experimental reports indicate moderate efficacy of rTMS in relieving the symptoms of depression and recovery from stroke. However, some researchers caution that the long-term risks associated with rTMS are unknown and that these must be subject to further study before its therapeutic use is considered acceptable. It is still unclear just how long lasting any beneficial therapeutic results of rTMS may be.

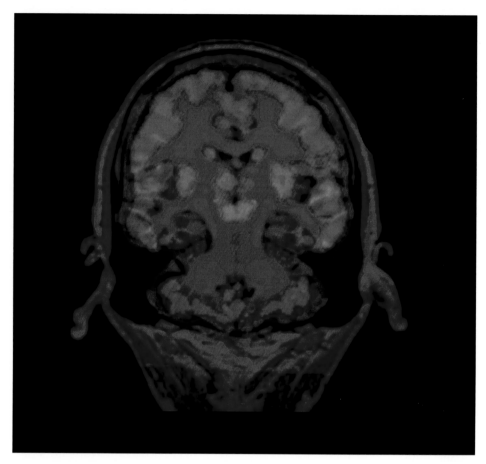

Coronal image of the brain obtained from a SPECT scan. *(Harry Sieplinga/HMS Images. Living Art Enterprises. Getty)*

ANIMAL STUDIES

The utility of rTMS as a means of altering brain activity in experiments has significant limitations. For example, currently its effects are limited to the outer layers of the brain and cortex. It is of little use in experiments aimed at delineating the function of components of the brain located deep beneath the cortex. When there is no compelling medical reason for a surgical intervention that would impact the integrity of the brain and its function, such as existed in the case of H.M., investigators rely on experiments with laboratory animals. Although non-human primates as well as other species have been used in these studies, rodents are the principle species that the majority of investigations employ. You may well wonder what legitimate value brain research using rats or mice may have for elucidating the functions of the human brain. Clearly, there are differences between our own brains and the brains of these animals (as well as differences in behaviors). Nonetheless, after decades of research with such animals, scientists can confirm that there are also remarkable similarities.

Invasive surgical procedures on the brains of laboratory rodents often utilize detailed neuroanatomical maps of brain structures and a devise called a stereotaxic frame. Using the stereotaxic frame and the neuroanatomical maps, investigators can perform very precise surgical procedures on anesthetized rodents that alter or record activity within specific neural structures and pathways. For example, they may implant an electrode that allows them to record activity as the animal performs some task or are exposed to some stimulus in their environment once they have regained consciousness and recovered from the implant surgery. Such studies reveal that there are at least three types of brain cells that help rodents navigate in their environment. *Head* cells keep track of what direction that animal's head is pointed. *Place* cells are most active when the animal is located within a specific place within its environment, and different *grid* cells are most active when the animal occupies a location that is best triangulated from the activity in three place cells. Researchers have recently identified cells that appear to function like place cells in humans. Although head and grid cells have yet to be identified in the human brain, think of how all three types of cells might help you navigate within a familiar environment.

Alternatively, investigators may surgically remove a portion of an animal's brain or severe a neural pathway connecting two regions of the brain and then observe the consequence(s) this has on the behavior of the animal. Such observation is generally relative to comparable observation of the behavior of a control group of animals that have undergone a sham surgical procedure (sham surgery involves all aspects of the experimental surgery except for the removal or disconnection of the neural tissue). Using this approach, investigators have found that surgical removal of neural tissue in regions of the brain that contain grid cells causes impairments in spatial navigation and inhibits animals from learning how to successfully negotiate various mazes.

Stereotaxic procedures also make it possible to implant a narrow tube (cannula) through which drugs may be administered once the animal is conscious. The effects of the drug on behavior are then compared to the animal's own behavior in the absence of the drug, or behaviors of a control group of animals. Infusion of a drug that temporarily inactivates neural activity through a cannula targeting the region of the rodent brain that contains grid cells has been found to impair the ability of the animals to acquire and retain spatial information needed to successfully navigate at least one type of maze.

These are examples of just several invasive surgical approaches that are commonly employed by investigators using animal models to gain a fuller understanding of how the brain is functionally organized. Animal models have also played an important role in furthering our understanding of the influence of genes on the expression of complex behavioral traits.

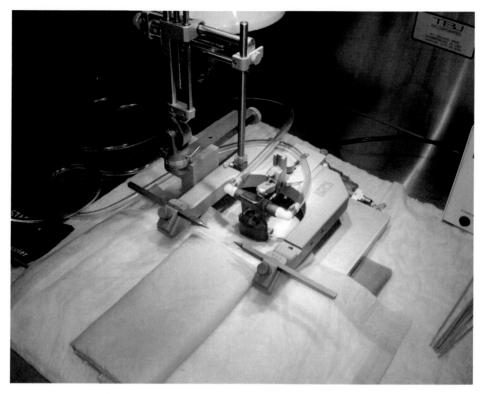

Stereotaxic surgical frame. *(Michael Kerchner)*

GENES AND BEHAVIOR

It is very likely that you may know someone who has a behavioral trait or a malady that is (at least in part) a product of heredity. In some cases, genes can contribute to expression of some extraordinary talent. Can you roll your tongue lengthwise? The ability to do so has been attributed to a single dominant gene. Are you among 75 percent of the population who are "super-tasters"? This trait is also attributed to a dominant gene. If you are among those who are unable to roll your tongue or are not super tasters, you have two copies of the recessive genes for these traits. Some of these traits exhibit patterns of inheritance that can be explained according to principles first described by Gregor Mendel in the 17th century.

Humans possess 23 pairs of chromosomes. The first 22 pairs (1 through 22) are classified as **autosomal chromosomes**. The genes that determine whether you can roll your tongue or are a super-taster are located on one of these autosomal pairs of chromosomes. The 23rd pair, the **sex chromosomes**, determines biological sex. Men have an X and a Y chromosome. Women have two copies of an X chromosome. When a recessive or dominant gene is located on one of these sex chromosomes, the gene's expression can differ (depending upon the sex of the individual).

If you are male, there is a 1 in 10 chance that you may have inherited a deficiency in the ability to perceive shades of green and red. If you are female, a deficiency in red-green color vision is much less likely. Most forms of red-green color blindness are due to an inherited variation in photoreceptors located in the retina of the eye, which result in an insensitivity to hues in the red-green portion of the color spectrum.

The red-green color deficiency is a recessive trait associated with genes found on the X chromosome. Females must inherit the gene responsible for red-green color blindness on each X chromosome. If one X chromosome has the gene for color-blindness and the other X chromosome does not, a female will not be color-blind. However, because males have just one X chromosome, a male who inherits a gene for color-blindness will be color-blind. The recessive character of the gene for the most common form of red-green color blindness and the fact that the gene is located on the X chromosome accounts for the more frequent occurrence of color-blindness among males. Similar explanations have been proposed for gender disparities observed in the relative risk that men and women have for some psychological and behavioral disorders.

Some disorders that affect the brain and nervous system also occur in the population in patterns indicating their transmission via Mendelian mechanisms inheritance. Among these are some very devastating neurological disorders. Folk musician Woody Guthrie was an exceptional and influential talent whose songs have inspired generations of songwriters and singers, including Bob Dylan and Wilco, a group that has released CDs featuring their own renditions of Guthrie's songs. In 1952, Guthrie was diagnosed with the dominant genetic neurodegenerative disorder that we know as **Huntington disease (HD).** Fifteen years later (in 1967) , he died from the disease. Over the course of those 15 years, the neurodegenerative effects of the disorder manifested itself in symptoms that progressively increased in severity. Early symptoms included problems with balance and coordination, involuntary facial tics, and mild cognitive impairment. These progressively and inexorably worsened and, in the years preceding his death, Guthrie experienced severe disturbances in balance and coordination, repetitive involuntary movements of limbs, muscular rigidity, difficulty swallowing, and dementia.

For reasons that remain unclear, the symptoms of Huntington disease (HD) result from the degeneration of neural tissue within selective regions of the brain, particularly within a set of structures known to serve important functions in the control of movement. These structures are collectively referred to as the *basal ganglia*. Like many disorders, HD is named after the physician who first described the symptoms of the disorder, George Huntington.

In the 1980s, Nancy Wexler was among a number of investigators conducting a detailed study of the inheritance patterns and genetic cause of HD among inhabitants of an island off the coast of Venezuela where there had been a very high incidence of HD. In 1993, Wexler's work led to the discovery of a gene for HD on chromosome 4 that reguates the production of a protein found within the brain that has been named *huntingtin*. A mutation affecting the HD gene leads to the production of an abnormal variant of the huntingtin protein, causing the degeneration of neurons in which the pathologic protein accumulates.

HD is a dominant gene disorder; if two copies of the HD gene are inherited, fetus death is inevitable. For offspring inheriting one HD gene, the odds may be very different. Woody Guthrie's children, including his songwriter-son Arlo Guthrie, each had either a 1 in 2 (50 percent) chance of inheriting the disorder. At the age of 63, Arlo is relatively healthy and has not experienced symptoms that would confirm inheritance of HD. Because the first symptoms of HD typically manifest themselves in people between the ages of 30 and 50, Arlo has apparently bested the odds.

The classic examples of dominant and recessive single-gene Mendelian traits do not appear to be highly influenced by the environment. In other words, whether you are color-blind or can roll your tongue or suffer from Huntington's does not seem to depend upon environmental factors. Moreover, you express the trait fully, or not at all.

But not all patterns of inheritance conform to those predicted by simple Mendelian mechanisms or can adequately be attributed to single-gene dominant versus recessive characterization. Geneticists have identified various exceptions to these simple mechanisms. Most complex physical and behavioral traits, particularly those emotional and cognitive abilities studied by psychologists, are influenced by many different genes and are often subject to modification by environmental factors. Because complex polygenetic traits generally manifest themselves along a continuum rather than simply by their presence or absence, such traits are referred to as *qualitative traits*, rather than *quantitative traits*. Would you consider eye-color to be a qualitative or a quantitative trait? If you identified eye color to be a qualitative trait, most people would probably agree with you because that is what has been taught in most introductory courses in biology or genetics. However, recent studies indicate that even eye color is subject to influences from numerous genes. As it happens, just as there are numerous variations in different shades of blue, green, and brown paints, there are similar variations in the colors of the iris in people's eyes, which are determined by complex interactions among numerous genes. Thus, some traits that were once thought to be qualitative may in fact be quantitative.

Among the complex quantitative traits of greatest interest to psychologists are those that contribute to such debilitating disorders as depression, anxiety, addiction, schizophrenia, autism, attention deficits, and dementia. Multiple genetic factors, as well as environmental factors, have been shown to be important aspects in determining the expression of each of these traits. Traditionally several approaches have been used to determine the relative contributions of genetic and environmental factors in expression of complex quantitative traits. Among these are family studies, twin studies, adoption studies, and linkage studies.

Consider chronic depression. It has long been recognized that risk of depressive disorders shows a pattern of inheritance within families, a fact that implicates significant contribution from genes. Although each person diagnosed as clinically depressed has core symptoms in common, even within a family such symptoms are also likely to be unique from each other in numerous and substantive ways. Some examples of possible distinctions are the age of onset, the presence or absence of suicidal thoughts, history of substance abuse, and differences in response to medications or therapeutic approaches in counseling. So how can the relative contribution of specific genes and environmental factors be determined in the case of clinical depression?

You should have a relatively good idea what is involved in family studies of complex traits. These studies rely on the careful construction of extensive and relatively complete family histories to document the occurrence of the trait among individual members of a family across several generations. The result is a family pedigree illustrating the relationships between affected and unaffected individuals within the family tree. Single-gene traits that follow simple Mendelian patterns of inheritance can be easily identified in these pedigrees. Patterns of inheritance that deviate from those predicted by Mendelian mechanisms are recognizable by default—if not Mendelian then some other! But, although traditional familial studies may be useful in distinguishing qualitative from quantitative traits, they are limited in their ability to identify and locate genes that contribute to quantitative traits. To refine this identification process, modern geneticist, aided by DNA mapping sequences, perform a **family-based linkage analysis**. As long as they have samples of DNA from members of the family who are included in the pedigree, geneticist can map the co-occurrence of the trait of interest and sequences of DNA in the affected members of the family that do not appear among the unaffected members. Initially, such analyses are useful in identifying segments of DNA on various chromosomes that may contain genes that contribute to the expression of the trait. As the cost of genomic screening has diminished, it has become feasible to expand such analyses to include entire populations. Such genome-wide linkage analysis may detect very rare genetic factors that family-based studies would not identify. In the foreseeable future, the accuracy of linkage analyses is likely to be vastly improved.

Twin studies that compare the presence of a trait among monozygotic (MZ) twins, dizygotic twins (DZ), siblings, and relatives of more distant relation have been helpful in estimating the relative contributions of genes and environment in expression of complex traits, including psychiatric disorders such as schizophrenia and depression. When two individuals share the same trait they are *concordant* for that trait. If genes alone primarily determine a trait, then MZ twins should always be concordant, i.e., there is 100 percent concordance among MZ twins. It would follow that 50 percent of DZ twins would be expected to be concordant for the same trait, i.e., both twins would be expected to express the

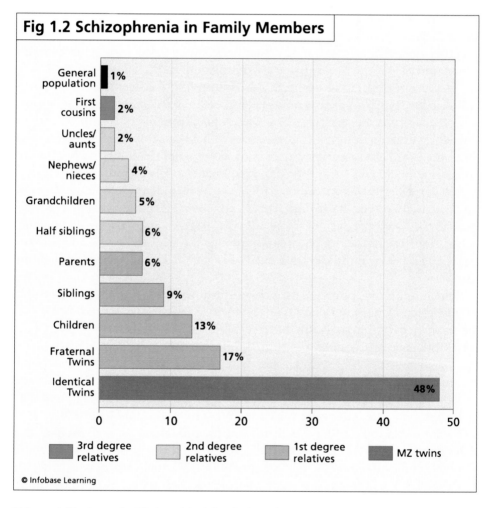

This graph illustrates the lifetime risk of developing schizophrenia in cases where a relative has been diagnosed with schizophrenia. Note that the degree to which any two individuals are related increases the proportion of genes in common. Nevertheless, the influence of environment is also a significant factor in determining risk of illness; even among identical twins, the risk is 50-50 that both twins will be schizophrenic.

trait in 50 out of 100 pairs. Pairs of siblings would also be concordant in 50 percent of the cases. And, as the degree of relatedness between individuals diminishes (e.g., cousins, nieces/nephews, etc.), the concordance rate should diminish proportionately.

Consider the pattern that has emerged in concordance rates for schizophrenia among individuals of various degrees of relatedness (see Figure 1.2). Note that the incidents of concordance between individuals follows the pattern expected if schizophrenia was a trait determined in part by genetic factors. But, the concordance among MZ twins is not 100 percent. Indeed, the concordance among identical twins is observed in approximately 50 percent of the pairs included in such studies. Clearly some factors besides genetics influence whether one MZ twin (or both or neither) is diagnosed with schizophrenia. These other factors are most likely environmental.

Adoption studies are useful in determining how influential environmental factors may be in determining the expression of a complex trait. Consider the case of orphaned MZ twins that are adopted into different families and are therefore raised in different environments. What impact would you predict this has on the concordance for a trait such as schizophrenia among MZ twins? What might you conclude if the observed incidence of concordance decreases? What if incidents of concordance increase? Which of these outcomes would indicate that environmental influences can either ameliorate genetic risks factors, exacerbated risk factors, or negate risk factors? And, what might you conclude if the incidence of concordance among adopted MZ twins adopted and reared by separate families was indistinguishable from MZ twins adopted into the same family?

Such adoption studies have generally shown that the environment can influence concordance among twins (sometimes decreasing concordance), but generally, environmental differences experienced by twins reared apart have little influence on concordance. But, although concordance for schizophrenia among identical twins appears relatively stable regardless of differences in environment, this does not mean that environment has no influence. Remember, in roughly half of all pairs of identical twins in which one twin is diagnosed with schizophrenia, the other twin is healthy. What may account for this?

One revelation that has resulted from the numerous genome projects that have been conducted during the past decade is that the expression of traits coded for by genes is often regulated by sequences of DNA that were once regarded to serve no obvious function. What for a time had been considered to be "junk" DNA is now recognized as serving a potentially important role in determining which genes are expressed, where in the body or brain genes are expressed, and when they are expressed. Thus, genome components that were once regarded as inconsequential are now known to comprise the **epigenome**. Furthermore, it has become increasingly evident that the epigenome plays a very important role in the interaction between environmental factors and the expression of genetic traits. Via its influence on the epigenome, the environment can determine what, where, and when genes may be expressed. Although MZ twins reared within the same household have very similar environmental experiences, their experiences are unlikely to be identical. For example, one of the twins may come down with flu, whereas the other twin may not. Likewise, even though they have shared the same womb, there may have been subtle differences in the fetal environment that impacted their epigenomes differently and thereby influenced the expression of divergent genetic traits very early in their development. Differences in epigenomic influences may explain why MZ twins who share the same genes may not express all these genes in the same manner throughout their lives and may be discordant rather than concordant for certain complex psychological and biobehavioral traits. Epigenomic influences may also account for the sporadic occurrence of a complex genetic trait in an individual whose family history would not indicate the likelihood of a given trait being expressed.

The exponential growth in our knowledge of the genome and epigenome has resulted in an increasing potential to manipulate the expression of the traits they regulate. For reasons that should be self-evident, experimentation in which investigators intentionally alter the genetic expression of traits in humans is ethically prohibited. There have been rare cases in which gene therapies have been implemented for the purpose of reversing or ameliorating certain severely debilitating or potentially lethal medical conditions. But in all instances, these have been preceded by extensive preliminary research employing genetically modified animals. One such approach utilizes Knock-out (KO) mice.

Knock-out mice are animals in which a functional segment of DNA (i.e., a gene) has been replaced with a non-function sequence of DNA. Just how this is done is beyond the scope of this discussion, but the result is that the normal influence of this gene has been negated in all of the genetically modified KO animals. Comparison of the behaviors of the KO mice to mice of the same strain that have not been genetically altered can provide a glimpse into the role that the gene expression normally has. Using information from linkage-analysis studies in humans to identify candidate genes that may contribute to the expression of symptoms characteristic of psychiatric disorders, and taking advantage of the fact that many genes that humans possess are also present in the genome of mice, investigators can create KO mice that lack these candidate genes and see what effect this creates. For example, a team of researchers working in Switzerland recently created a KO mouse lacking a functional gene needed for production of a protein found in some brain cells. The salient point here is that this protein is deficient in the same cells in the brains of schizophrenics. Testing indicated that the behaviors of the KO mice shared some similarities with behaviors characteristic of schizophrenics. The KO mice displayed abnormalities in the way that they processed sensory stimuli, they tended to engage in repetitive stereotyped behaviors, and they showed an increased sensitivity to the effects of a drug that exacerbates the symptoms of schizophrenics and produces hallucinations in healthy humans who ingest higher than prescribed levels of this medication.

In the example above, whether the investigator created mice that were schizophrenic or not does not matter. What does matter is that this study provides further evidence for the probable role of the specific gene that these investigators manipulated and the protein that the gene normally expresses in the pathology of schizophrenia. It is very likely that there are numerous genes and epigenetic factors that interact in the case of schizophrenia. Nonetheless, future studies with such KO animals may lead to therapeutic interventions that will be effective in treating some symptoms of schizophrenia in humans.

INSTITUTIONAL REVIEW BOARDS (IRBS), INSTITUTIONAL ANIMAL CARE AND USE COMMITTEES (IACUCS), AND RESEARCH ETHICS

It is important to note that all experimental investigations that employ human and animal subjects are reviewed by committees prior to their implementation to insure that they are consistent with contemporary research guidelines. These guidelines were established to meet societal ethical standards of conduct and were created to protect human participants and/or animal subjects from unacceptable risks or discomfort and pain. One dominant feature of these guidelines is that human participants must be fully informed of the potential risks as well as the benefits of the research; another is that investigators must obtain the consent of participants to engage in a study before the study begins. In the case of animal research or research with young human children, informed consent cannot be assumed. The standards that investigators are held to in these instances are much higher, and there are additional requirements for oversight in such studies to ensure that the research is methodologically sound and ethical, and that the potential benefits to society are adequate justification given that informed consent may be impossible to obtain.

Further Reading

American Psychological Association (APA). Responsible Conduct of Research. Available at http://www.apa.org/research/responsible/index.aspx. Retrieved November 2011.

Corkin, S. "What's New with the Amnesic Patient H.M? *Nature Reviews Neuroscience* 3 (2002): 153–160.

Fields. R.D. (April 2011). "The Hidden Brain." *Scientific American Mind,* 22 (April 2011): 52–59.

Fleischman, J. *A Gruesome But True Story about Brain Science.* Boston, Mass.: Houghton Mifflin, 2002.

Huntington's Outreach Project for Education [Stanford University]. Available at http://hopes.stanford.edu/home. Retrieved November 2011.

Institute for Laboratory Animal Research (ILAR). Available at http://dels.nas.edu/ilar. Retrieved November 2011.

Malcolm Macmillan's Phineas Gage Information Site. Available at http://www.deakin.edu.au/hmnbs/psychology/gagepage/. Retrieved November 2011.

Society For Neuroscience "Brain Briefings." Available at http://www.sfn.org/index.aspx?pagename=brainbriefings_main. Retrieved November 2011.

NOVA Epigenetics. Available at http://www.pbs.org/wgbh/nova/body/epigenetics.html. Retrieved November 2011.

NOVA Science NOW: The Man Who Couldn't Remember. Available at http://www.pbs.org/wgbh/nova/body/corkin-hm-memory.html. Retrieved November 2011.

NOVA The Secret Life of the Brain. Available at http://www.pbs.org/wnet/brain/index.html. Retrieved November 2011.

Ridding, M.C., and Rothwell, J.C. "Is There a Future for Therapeutic Use of Transcranial Magnetic Stimulation?" *Nature Reviews. Neuroscience,* 8(2007): 559–567.

Ridley, M. *Nature via Nurture. Genes, Experience, and What Makes Us Human.* New York, N.Y: Harper Collins, 2003.

Sacks, O. *The Man Who Mistook His Wife for a Hat and Other Clinical Tales.* New York N.Y.: Touchstone, 1998.

UC San Diego Brain Observatory. Available at http://thebrainobservatory.ucsd.edu/. Retrieved November 2011.

Woman's Long-Term Memory Astonishes Scientists. Available at http://www.npr.org/templates/story/story.php?storyId=5350362. Retrieved November 2011.

CHAPTER 2

CELLULAR PHYSIOLOGY OF THE NERVOUS SYSTEM FUNCTION

NEURONS AND GLIA

The nervous system actually comprises several different systems, each specialized for specific functions. The two main systems are the central nervous system (CNS) and the peripheral nervous system (PNS). The CNS consists of the brain and spinal cord, which are encased in the skull and vertebral column, respectively. The PNS includes all nervous tissue outside the skull and vertebral column and comprises two branches: the somatic system and the autonomic system. We will return to consider the functional organization and specialization of these systems, but first we will examine the unique properties of their cells—neurons and glia.

The cells of each organ are specialized for the function that the organ serves. Lung tissue is specialized to perform the functions of breathing and respiration. Cells in kidneys are specialized for excreting urine. The cells that comprise the nervous system are specialized for rapidly conveying bioelectrical signals—neural signals—between various organ systems. The cells that enable this are neurons, and the cells that assist their function are called glia.

Figure 2.1 illustrates the key components of a neuron. There is a cell body (soma) containing the cell's nucleus and numerous cellular organelles (e.g., mitochondria and ribosomes), as well as multiple dendrites and an axon that extends from the soma, forming a network of interconnections with other neurons as well as with organs and tissues. The signal that a neuron generates travels

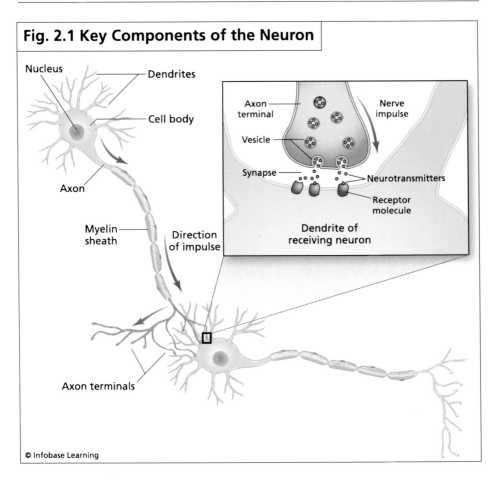

Key components of a neuron.

from the cell body along the axon. The end of the axon extends toward another receiving neuron and communicates with that neuron across a microscopic gap called a synapse. Synaptic junctions may occur between an axon and the soma of another neuron, i.e., axo-somatic synapses. But other synaptic arrangements may also occur. For example, axon-axonal synapses occur between the axon of one neuron and the axon of another neuron, and axon-dendritic synapses occur between an axon and the dendrites of a receiving neuron. The potential complexity of the interactions among neurons is staggering. Nerves are essentially bundles of axons of many neurons. And larger assemblies of nerves form fiber tracts.

Several types of glial cells are found in close association with neurons. Some glial cells envelop the axon in a sheath, providing structural support but also facilitating the speed at which neural signals travel along the axon. This sheath or **myelin** is composed primarily of lipids that insulate the axon. The glia that form the myelin sheath in the CNS are called **oligodendroglia**; whereas **Schwann cells** form myelin in the PNS.

In addition to oligodendroglia and Schwann cells, there are many other glial cells that contribute both structural and functional support within the CNS and PNS. Until relatively recently, the full extent of the contributions that glia have with respect to healthy functioning of the nervous system were underestimated. The term glia is derived from the Greek term that means "glue," but it is now clear that glia serve many more functions than their name would imply. Two other types of glia, microglia and astrocytes, are found throughout the brain and spinal cord and are also capable of communicating with one another, with neurons, and helping to coordinate processes to limit or repair damage resulting form neural trauma and disease. The declining ability of glia to perform such functions over a lifetime may increase vulnerability to various neurodegenerative disorders as we age; in some instances, glia may actively contribute to the neurodegenerative processes associated with illnesses such as AIDS/HIV, **Amyotrophic Lateral Sclerosis** (ALS; also known as Lou Gehrig's Disease) and Alzheimer's disease.

THE RESTING AND ACTION POTENTIAL

The bioelectric signal that is transmitted from the soma along the axon is called the action potential. Between each action potential the neuron is at relative rest, but even during this period the neuron is selectively shuttling positively and negatively charged ions across its cell membrane, resulting in a difference in the electrical charge between the inside and outside of the neuron. This resulting difference in the concentration of charged ions within the neuron and in the extracellular space surrounding it is approximately negative 50 to 80 millivolts (mV). This is the resting potential of the neuron. To understand how the resting potential contributes to the action potential of the cell requires a deeper examination of the mechanisms that contribute to the unequal distribution of charged ions.

The Resting Potential

The membrane of the neuron is semi-permeable, meaning that some constituents in the cytoplasm and the extracellular space surrounding the membrane may not cross the membrane unless this occurs via an active transport mechanism. The transport mechanisms that are found in the axonal membrane of neurons are actually protein constituents of the cellular membrane. These proteins selectively bind to specific ions and transport them from the extracellular space into the cytoplasm and/or transport them from inside the neuron to the extracellular space. The resting potential of the cell is chiefly the result of one such transporter that expels approximately three sodium ions ($Na+$) from the interior of the neuron in exchange for one potassium ion (K+) which it draws into the neuron. For reasons that should be apparent, this transporter is called a sodium-potassium pump. There are several other charged ions that are unequally distributed on the inside and outside of the neuron and also contribute to the resting potential. For example, while the neuron is at rest, chloride (Cl-) ions and calcium (Ca2+) are in higher concentration outside the neuron than within it. But if we account for the concentration of all the positive and negative charged ions on either side of the cell membrane when the neuron is at rest, the difference in charges equate to the resting potential of the neuron, and the interior of the neuron is negatively charged relative to the outside of the neuron, i.e., -50 to -80 mV.

The Action Potential and Its Axonal Transmission

The unequal distribution of charged ions at rest establish disequilibrium gradients in two forces. The electrostatic force, the difference in the charges across the membrane, tends to draw positive ions into the interior of the cell if the permeability of the membrane allows this. Additionally, if the permeability of the membrane allows, osmotic force—the difference in the concentration gradient of each ion—tends to draw ions that are in higher concentration outside the cell into the cell, and those ions in higher concentration inside the cell are transmitted outside the cell.

What would happen if the permeability of the membrane were to change and allow only Na+ ions to cross the membrane unimpeded? Look carefully at Table 2.1 before you answer.

The inside of the neuron at rest is negatively charged, therefore if Na+ ions were unimpeded, they would flow along their electrostatic gradient, from the positively charged extracellular space to the negatively charged intracellular space until an equilibrium in charges was established. Similarly, the osmotic gradient would also draw Na+ ions into the interior of the neuron until the relative concentration of Na+ on either side of the neuronal membrane was in equilibrium.

Such a change in the permeability of the neuronal membrane to Na+ is what initiates an action potential, i.e., the neural signal that moves from the soma along the axon to the synapse. If the neuronal membrane were to suddenly allow Na+ ions to cross unimpeded, Na+ ions would rush into the neuron, inevitably making the interior of the neuron more positively charged than when at rest. Because the osmotic force is greater than the electrostatic force, the interior of the neuron actually becomes more positively charged relative to the outside, often reaching a peak of +50 to 70 mV.

The mechanism that allows for the sudden shift in membrane permeability for Na+ described above is the result of protein channels in the membrane that

TABLE 2.1

The Relative Extracellular and Intracellular Concentrations of Key Ions Found During the Resting Potential of a Typical Neuron (-70mV).

	Sodium (Na+)	Potassium (K+)	Calcium (Ca+)	Anions
Extracellular Concentration	High	Low	High	Low
Direction of Osmotic Force	↓	↑	↓	↑
Direction of Electrostatic Force	↓	↓	↓	↑
Intracellular Concentration	Low	High	Low	High

are either closed or open, depending upon the charge across the membrane. These are called voltage gated Na+ channels.

Here is how voltage gated Na+ channels in an axon are opened. When one neuron receives an excitatory signal from another neuron, the arriving signal causes the membrane of the receiving neuron to become slightly depolarized, e.g., from -70 mV to -60 mV. At this point the voltage gated Na+ channels that have been closed, suddenly open, thereby allowing Na+ ions to rush into the neuron and rapidly altering the relative charge across the membrane. The interior of the neuron is now more positively charged than the outside, reaching a peak of +50 mV. The voltage gated Na+ channels now close.

At this point a second set of voltage gated channels, which until now have been closed, open. These channels selectively allow K+ ions to move across the membrane, following existing osmotic and electrostatic gradients. The osmotic and electrostatic forces now cause K+ ions to rush from the interior of the neuron into the extracellular space. Inevitably, this causes the charge across the membrane to reverse once again, eventually reaching and overshooting the original resting potential and thereby hyperpolarizing the neuron. At this point the voltage gated K+ channels close once again, allowing the Na+/K+ pump to reestablish the resting potential of the neuron.

The mechanisms that contribute to the action potential are summarized in Figure 2.2. The entire event, from the point the action potential is generated until the point that the resting potential is reestablished, takes between 2.5 and 3 milliseconds.

Now consider what the consequence would be if someone were exposed to a toxin that blocks voltage gated Na+ channels. What effect would this have on the generation of action potentials in the person's nervous system? In fact there

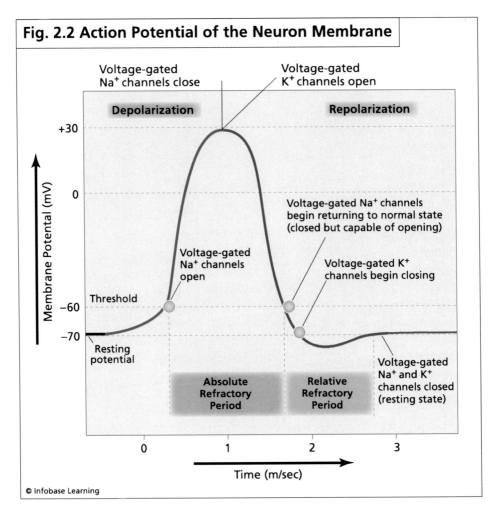

Fig. 2.2 Action Potential of the Neuron Membrane

Voltage-gated
Na⁺ channels close

Voltage-gated
K⁺ channels open

Depolarization

Repolarization

+30

0

Voltage-gated Na⁺ channels
begin returning to normal state
(closed but capable of opening)

Voltage-gated
Na⁺ channels
open

Voltage-gated K⁺
channels begin closing

Threshold

−60

−70

Resting
potential

Voltage-gated
Na⁺ and K⁺
channels closed
(resting state)

**Absolute
Refractory
Period**

**Relative
Refractory
Period**

Membrane Potential (mV)

0   1   2   3

Time (m/sec)

© Infobase Learning

The sequence of events that alter the neuronal membranes' permeability to Na+ and K+ during an action potential. Once the charge across the membrane of the neuron reaches the threshold of excitation, voltage gated Na+ channels open, allowing Na+ to flow into the neuron, which causes the charge to rise and become positive. At the peak in the action potential, Na+ channels close, and voltage gated K+ channels open. K+ then flow into the neuron, making the extracellular space more negatively charged (lowering the extracellular concentration of K+). Eventually the K+ channels close, and the Na+/K+ pump restores the original distribution of Na+ and K+ ions, reestablishing the resting potential.

are several neurotoxins that are voltage gated Na+ channel blockers. For example, the liver and ovaries of some puffer fish (*Tetraodontidae*) contain **tetrodotoxin (TTX)**, a Na+ channel blocker. Since the puffer fish is a sushi delicacy, care must be taken in preparing the dish so that none of the meal contains TTX. Occasionally, some people who have the misfortune of consuming improperly prepared puffer-fish sushi end up in hospital emergency rooms. Because there is no effective antidote, the outcome depends upon the dose consumed, the time it took to receive emergency care, and the effectiveness of steps taken by the hospital staff to eliminate TTX from the body.

The origin of the axon potential typically takes place at the axon hilloc, located at the juncture of the neuronal soma and the axon. From this site, the action potential moves along the axon in the direction of the synapse. The speed of axonal transmission of the action potential is facilitated by the myelin sheath. The speed of axonal transmission along a myelinated axon can exceed the speed that is possible along a non-myelinated axon. Another factor influencing the speed of axonal transmission is the diameter of the axon. The greater the diameter, the faster axonal transmission occurs. Typical speeds range from 1 meter per second up to and slightly exceeding 100 meters per second.

PNS: CRANIAL NERVES, SPINAL NERVES, AND SOMATIC AND AUTONOMIC NERVOUS SYSTEMS

There are twelve cranial nerves in the PNS that originate directly from the base of the brain. Some serve solely afferent (sensory) functions; some serve solely efferent (motor) function, e.g., controlling contraction of smooth or striated muscles or the activity of some glands. Four of the cranial nerves serve both sensory and motor functions. The names and primary functions of the twelve cranial nerves are listed in Table 2.2.

The nerves that comprise the efferent fibers of the PNS originate from the spinal cord, as do the corresponding afferent fibers. There are a total of 31 spinal nerves, each one emerging from within each segment of the spinal vertebra: 8 cervical, 12 thoracic, 5 lumbar, 5 sacral, and 1 coccygeal. The afferent fibers enter the spinal cord via the dorsal (closest to the back) root of each spinal nerve, whereas the efferent fibers exit the spinal cord via the ventral (closest to the abdomen) root of each spinal nerve.

Each spinal nerve contains fibers that are components of the somatic or the autonomic branches of the PNS. The somatic branch contains afferent and efferent fibers that innervate skeletal muscles. In some textbooks, the somatic nervous system is described as coordinating voluntary movements and action. However, involuntary movements are also mediated by the somatic system. The most obvious illustration of this is the "knee-jerk:" or patellar reflex that is a common component of the typical physical examination. Both voluntary and involuntary reflexive movements of the lower leg are mediated by the somatic

TABLE 2.2

The Twelve Cranial Nerves and Their Functions

Cranial Nerve		Function
I	Olfactory	Olfaction (sensory)
II	Optic	Vision (sensory)
III	Oculomotor	Eye movements (motor)
IV	Trochlear	Eye movements (motor)
V	Trigeminal	Face and teeth (sensory); jaw (motor)
VI	Abducens	Eye movements (motor)
VII	Facial	Facial, tongue and soft palate (sensory); Facial muscles, salivary glands and tear ducts (motor)
VIII	Vestibulocochlear	Balance and hearing (sensory)
IX	Glossopharyngeal	Taste and oral sensations (sensory); Throat muscles (motor)
X	Vagus	Introceptive sensations (sensory); internal organs (motor)
XI	Spinal accessory	Muscles of the neck (motor)
XII	Hypoglossal	Tongue muscles (motor)

system. The autonomic branch of the PNS is itself composed of two branches, the parasympathetic and the sympathetic systems. Although the autonomic system is often regarded as mediating involuntary and/or unconscious actions, this too is not always the case as some autonomic functions (e.g., heart rate, blood pressure) may be consciously controlled with the aid of biosensors and biofeedback training.

The parasympathetic branch of the autonomic system generally regulates organ systems such as the respiratory and digestive systems during periods rest, and energy conservation or storage. Activity within the parasympathetic system tends to slow heart rate, lower blood pressure, facilitate digestion, and stimulate salivation. However, during periods that require the expenditure of energy, the sympathetic branch of the autonomic system is activated. Activity within the sympathetic system tends to increase heart rate, raise blood pressure, and inhibit digestion and salivation.

Further Reading

Bean, B.P. "The Action Potential in Mammalian Central Neurons." *Nature Reviews Neuroscience* 8 (2007): 451–465.

Carlson, N.R. *Physiology of Behavior.* 10th ed. New York, N.Y.: Allyn & Bacon, 2010.

Carter, R. *The Human Brain Book.* New York, N.Y.: DK Publishing, 2009.

Howard Hughes Medical Institute (HHMI) Virtual Neurophysiology Lab. Available at http://www.hhmi.org/biointeractive/vlabs/neurophysiology/index.html. Retrieved November 2011.

Neuroscience for Kids. Available at http://faculty.washington.edu/chudler/neurok.html. Retrieved November 2011.

YouTube. Available at http://youtu.be/SCasruJT-DU. Retrieved November 2011.

CHAPTER 3

THE ROLE OF HORMONES AND NEUROTRANSMITTERS IN BEHAVIOR

Besides neurotransmitters, the other major chemical messengers are hormones. The primary sources of hormones are the endocrine glands (See Table 3.1), although the brain itself produces some neuroactive hormones locally. Indeed, the brain itself may be considered an endocrine gland. To gain an understanding of the endocrine nature of the brain requires a brief discussion of the hypothalamic-pituitary-adrenal (HPA) axis (see Figure 3.1).

THE HYPOTHALAMIC-PITUITARY-ADRENAL AXIS

The hypothalamus is located roughly in the center of the brain, just below the thalamus. The hypothalamus itself consists of numerous nuclei that collectively serve an important role in regulating such fundamental physiological processes as metabolism, body temperature, fluid balance, arousal, and reproduction. As a consequence, nuclei within the hypothalamus mediate motivational states such as hunger, thirst, fear, aggression, sleep, stress, and sexual arousal. This is accomplished (in part) via the regulation of hormone production and release, first from the pituitary gland and then from other endocrine glands, such as the adrenals. The pattern of hormone production and release is regulated by both negative and positive feedback within the HPA. For example, stressful circumstances trigger adaptive increases in adrenal hormones such as cortisol through positive feedback within the HPA. The result is increased production of Corticotropin Releasing Hormone (CRH) within the hypothalamus. CRH is

(continues on page 38)

TABLE 3.1

Major Endocrine Glands, Hormones, and Their Functions

Endocrine Gland	Primary Hormone(s)	Primary Function(s)
Pineal Gland	Melatonin	
Hypothalamus	Corticotropin Releasing Hormone (CRH)	Stimulates production of ACTH
	Gonadotropin Releasing Hormone (GnRH)	Stimulates production of LH and FSH
	Somatostatin (Growth Hormone Inhibiting Hormone)	Inhibits Somatotropin release
	Hypocretin (Orexin)	Regulates sleep & metabolism
Posterior Pituitary	Oxytocin	Reproductive processes (e.g. uterine contractions; suckling reflex in women)
	Vasopressin (Antidiuretic Hormone)	Regulates blood pressure & urination
Anterior Pituitary	Adrenocorticotropic Hormone (ACTH)	Stimulates cortisol release from adrenal cortex
	Somatotropin (Growth Hormone)	Bone & muscle growth
	Thyroid Stimulating Hormone (TSH)	Regulates metabolism
	Luteinizing Hormone (LH)	Gonadal hormone secretion
	Follicle Stimulating Hormone (FSH)	Gonadal hormone secretion
Thyroid	Thyroxine	Calcium metabolism
Parathyroids	Parathyroid Hormone (PTH) & Calcitonin (CT)	Promotes (PTH) & inhibits (CT) calcium metabolism
Adrenals	Cortisol Aldosterone	Stress/Immune response Fluid/Ion balance
Pancreas	Insulin	Liver glycogen storage & glucose utilization
	Glucagon	Conversion of glycogen to glucose
Ovaries	Estrogens, Progestins, Androgens	Reproduction
Testes	Androgens, Estrogens, Progestins,	Reproduction

Fig. 3.1 The Hypothalamic-Pituitary-Adrenal (HPA) Axis

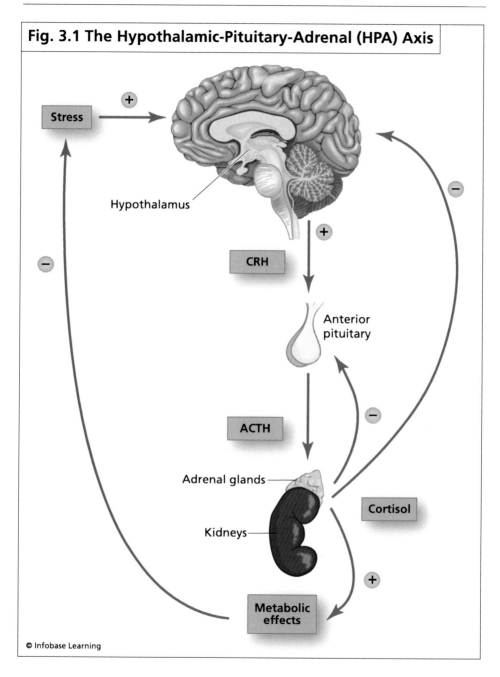

© Infobase Learning

A diagrammatic illustration of the hypothalamic-pituitary-adrenal (HPA) axis. Factors contributing to the release of cortisol from the adrenal glands are indicated by plus (+). Inhibitory influences on cortisol release via negative feedback are indicated by minus (-). CRH = Corticotropin Releasing Hormone; ACTH = Adrenocorticotropic Hormone.

(continued from page 35)
transported via a fine plexus of capillaries to the anterior pituitary, where CRH triggers increased production of Adrenocorticotropic Hormone (ACTH) from the pituitary. As levels of ACTH in the circulation rise, this triggers production and release of cortisol from the adrenal cortex. Once cortisol levels rise, negative feedback within the HPA limits further production of CRH and ACTH, and cortisol levels decline once more toward their original baseline.

Have you ever considered that just waking up in the morning may be a stressor? In fact, positive feedback in the HPA coordinates a steep increase in circulating levels of cortisol roughly 30 minutes after you awaken each morning. Within hours, the levels of cortisol decline again toward their baseline, only to increase once again late in the afternoon, before returning to baseline prior to bedtime.

Investigators have learned that depression is associated with sustained elevated levels of cortsol. Although not all depressed individuals show such an altered daily pattern of cortisol secretion across days and weeks, this may indicate that either a chronic stressor or dysregulation of the HPA axis contributes to depression. Some studies have found that the elevated levels of cortisol in depression may result from a deficit in the negative feedback. Interestingly, one of the diagnostic symptoms of depression is disruption of sleep (i.e., either insomnia or hypresomnia). It is conceivable that the absence of the normal circadian (daily) rhythm in cortisol secretion that is experienced by some depressed individuals may contribute to the disruption in patterns of sleep. Another neuroendocrine structure located with the brain that assists in regulating sleep is the pineal. The pineal produces the hormone melatonin, which normally peaks just prior to bedtime.

THE HYPOTHALAMIC-PITUITARY-GONDAL AXIS
Similar mechanisms regulate the production of hormones within the male and female reproductive system. This is the Hypothalamic-Pituitary-Gonadal Axis (HPG). In this case, production of gonadal hormones (from the testes or the ovaries) is controlled by the secretion of inhibiting and releasing hormones from the hypothalamus. As the terms imply, these either inhibit or promote the release of pituitary hormones, and thereby control the production of hormones by the gonads. Neuroendocrine cells in the hypothalamus produce Gonadotropin Releasing Hormone (GnRH). In response to peaks in GnRH the anterior pituitary releases Luteinizing Hormone (LH) and Follicle Stimulating Hormone (FSH). In males, LH promotes the production of testosterone by the testes. In women, LH promotes a peak in production of estrogen at mid-cycle that serves to promote ovulation. In men, FSH promotes spermatogenesis, whereas in women FSH fosters maturation of ovarian follicle (egg) and, together with LH, peaks prior to ovulation.

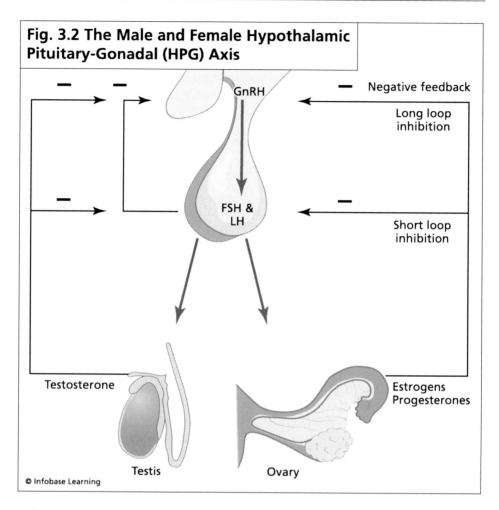

Fig. 3.2 The Male and Female Hypothalamic Pituitary-Gonadal (HPG) Axis

A diagram illustration of the male and female hypothalamic-pituitary-gonadal (HPG) axis. The male HPG is illustrated on the left and the female HPG on the right. In both instances, positive (red arrows) and negative (black minuses) feedback regulates circulating levels of the gonadal hormones. Differences in the HPG timing of positive and negative feedback mechanisms in men and women account for the differences in their reproductive cycles.

The importance of the hypothalamus in the regulation of endocrine hormones is evident in the different patterns of gonadal hormone production in postpubertal men and women. In women, the menstrual cycle[1] is coordinated

---

1. The term menstrual cycle refers specifically to its visible manifestation, menstruation. The same cycle could also be appropriately named the ovulatory cycle.

by a pattern of activity within the HPG axis that occurs over 26 to 28 days, with a peak in GnRH, LH, and FSH that occurs approximately at mid-cycle. In contrast, the hypothalamus in males produces a pulsatile spike in GnRH, LH, and FSH that occurs at intervals of roughly 45 minutes throughout each day. Differences in the HPG timing of positive and negative feedback mechanisms in men and women account for the differences in their reproductive cycles.

VASOPRESSIN, OXYTOCIN, AND AFFILIATIVE BONDS

Two neuroendocrine hormones that have attracted a great deal of attention in the last decade are vasopressin (VP) and oxytocin (OXT). Increases in these hormones have been associated with the formation of social bonds between individuals. Specialized neuroendocrine cells in the hypothalamus that project directly into the posterior pituitary produce vasopressin and oxytocin. One function of VP is to promote retention of fluid by inhibiting urination. OXT promotes uterine contractions in pregnant women at the time of birth. In women who are breast-feeding, release of oxytocin (OXT) triggers the expression of milk from their breast. Further investigation has indicated that the release of VP and/or OXT may facilitate the formation of the bond between parent and infant. The original evidence of the role of VP in formation of pair-bonds was obtained in experiments comparing neuroendocrine differences between rodents who formed stable monogamous mating pairs and rodents that mated with multiple partners. A surge in VP seemed to be essential for the formation of the monogamous bond. Moreover, the hypothalamus of the monogamous voles contained a dense concentration of receptors for VP, whereas the hypothalamus of the non-monogamous rodents contained comparatively few VP receptors. The same VP receptors, the *AVP1AR* receptor, that are implicated in the formation of monogamous rodent pair-bonds are also found in the human brain. However, the particular type of VP receptor that is expressed in any individual depends upon which of three different genes they inherit. In 2008, a team of researchers in Europe and the United States found that men who inherited two copies of a specific VP gene, RS3-334, perceived the strength of their relationship with their partners to be weaker in comparison to the perceptions of men who inherited alternate forms of the same gene. The partners of these RS3-335 men also rated the strength of their relationship less positively than the partners of the men who possessed other variants of the VP gene. Variants in the human VP gene have also been implicated in autism, a disorder that is characterized by difficulty in forming social bonds and impairments in empathy.

Experiments with human participants have found that OXT may also facilitate empathy, perceptions of trust, and social bonds between individuals. Elevations in circulating levels of OXT have been found to occur not just in new mothers but early in fatherhood as well. In one study in which college students received either a nasal spray containing OXT or a placebo prior to engaging in a monetary game with strangers whom they had to trust with their money, the participants who received the OXT were much more likely to entrust a greater sum of their money to the strangers than those who were administered the placebo. In another study, intranasal OXT was found to facilitate memory for familiar faces, but not familiar objects.

Other endocrine glands, the hormones they produce, and their functions are listed in Table 3.1. However, there are two atypical endocrine regulators that should be mentioned. These two examples illustrate that there may be a vast array of endocrine messages that originate from organs other than the traditional endocrine glands. These endocrine regulators are leptin and ghrelin. Both play important roles in the regulation of hunger, satiety, and obesity.

LEPTIN, GHRELIN, AND REGULATION OF BODY WEIGHT

As you may have heard, there is an ongoing crisis in the proportion of individuals in the United States who are obese. This battle of the bulge has launched intensive research into the neuroendocrine factors that may place some individuals at elevated risk for obesity and disorders, such as diabetes, that are associated with obesity. More than a decade ago, research examining a specific strain of mutant mice that were prone to excessive weight gain identified a chemical messenger in their circulation that was found in much higher concentrations than in their lean littermates. This chemical messenger was **leptin (LPTN).** However, another strain of mutant mice that were also prone to becoming extremely obese was found to have exceptionally low circulating levels of LPTN. These apparent contradictory findings were eventually resolved when it was determined that the mice with elevated levels of LPTN, the *db/db* mutants, were insensitive to LPTN, whereas the other strain of obese mutants was incapable of producing LPTN. When the latter group of obese mice, the *ob/ob* strain, was treated with injections of LPTN, they lost their excessive weight. Almost immediately, investigators raced to determine whether extremely obese humans might be either LPTN deficient like the *ob/ob* mice, or LPTN insensitive, like the *db/db* mice. If such morbidly obese individuals were like the *ob/ob* mice, then they might benefit from treatments that would increase circulating levels of LPTN in their blood. Unfortunately, the vast majority of morbidly obese individuals were determined to be insensitive to LPTN.

Subsequent research identified the source of LPTN to be adipose (white) fat. And LPTN receptors were localized in the hypothalamus of *ob/ob* mice. Thus, current evidence supports the hypothesis that circulating levels of LPTN are a means for the brain to gauge how much reserve energy resource is available as fat. Normally, hunger is suppressed and metabolism adjusted when LPTN levels rise as the proportion of body mass that comprises fat increases, thereby maintaining body weights within a normally healthy range. When fat reserves of energy become depleted, circulating levels of LPTN decline, facilitating hunger and adjusting metabolism to favor the conversion of excess calories as fat. For reasons that are as yet unknown, but which may be associated with the nature of our current lifestyles and diets, it may be that many individuals are becoming relatively insensitive to LPTN.

According to the hypothesis outlined above, obesity is associated with impairments in a mechanism that should limit consumption of food and conversion of excess calories into fat. An alternative hypothesis is that obesity may be associated with an increase in mechanisms that facilitate hunger, even when there is no need for additional caloric intake. This might be the case if there were an endocrine signal that would elicit hunger and encourage consumption of excess calories. As it happens, investigators have identified a chemical signal that fits this description and originates from specialized endocrine cells in the stomach. These cells produce **ghrelin** when the stomach is empty or when the nutritional value of the stomach contents is particularly poor. Ghrelin receptors are located in the hypothalamus and some ghrelin is produced locally within the hypothalamus. Circulating levels of ghrelin are elevated during fasting and are positively correlated with subjective feelings of hunger. Although levels of ghrelin typically decline after a meal, studies have shown that this is less likely among obese individuals.

Prader-Willi Syndrome (PWS) is a rare genetic disorder that affects children and is characterized by moderate developmental delay and impairments in learning, poor muscle tone, and poor motor coordination. As the disorder progresses these children may also exhibit ravenous patterns of binging and indiscriminant feeding, often resorting to pica (consumption of non-nutritive substances including dirt, feces, pebbles, etc.), and, if their diets and access to foods are not restricted, they gain weight. Studies have shown that children with PWS have elevated levels of circulating ghrelin but there may be other factors that reduce their responsiveness to signals that would normally induce satiety.

A brief note of caution is in order considering the limited scope of this description of hormonal factors regulating hunger, satiety, and body weight. Investigators have identified many other chemical messengers that ultimately influence our eating habits and an individual's risk of becoming obese or anorexic. Other hormones and various neurotransmitter systems also influence our patterns of eating, our basal metabolism, and ultimately, our body weight. Additionally, environmental and social factors can exert a significant influence.

Further Reading

Carter, C.S., and L.L. Getz. "Monogomy and the Prairie Vole." *Scientific American* 268, no. 6 (June 1992): 100–106.

Feldman, R., A. Weller, O Zagoory-Sharon, and A. Levine, A. "Evidence for a Neuroendocrinological Foundation of Human Affiliation: Plasma Oxytocin Levels Across Pregnancy and the Postpartum Period Predict Mother-Infant Bonding. *Psychological Science* 18, no. 11 (2007): 965–970.

Flier, J.S., and E. Maratos-Flier. "What Fuels Fat." *Scientific American* 297 (September 2007): 72–81.

Howard Hughes Medical Institute Holiday Lecture (2004): *The Science of Fat.* Available at http://www.hhmi.org/biointeractive/obesity/lectures.html. Retrieved November 2011.

Insel, T.R., and L.J. Young. "The Neurobiology of Attachment." *Nature Reviews Neuroscience* 2 (2001): 129–136.

Kuchinskas, S. *The Chemistry Connection: How the Oxytocin Response Can Help You Find Trust, Intimacy, and Love.* Oakland, Calif.: New Harbinger, 2009.

Lupien, S.J., B.S. McEwen, M.R. Gunnar, and C. Heim. "Effects of Stress Throughout the Lifespan on the Brain, Behavior, and Cognition." *Nature Reviews Neuroscience* 10 (2009): 434–445.

Nelson, R.J. *An Introduction to Behavioral Endocrinology.* 4th ed. Sunderland, Mass.: Sinauer, 2011.

NIH Prader-WIlli Syndrome Information. Available at http://www.nichd.nih.gov/health/topics/Prader_Willi_Syndrome.cfm. Retrieved November 2011.

Zak, P.J. "The Neurobiology of Trust." *Scientific American* 298 (June 2008): 88–95.

CHAPTER 4

SENSORY AND PERCEPTUAL SYSTEMS

"If real is what you can feel, smell, taste and see, then 'real' is simply electrical signals interpreted by your brain." Morpheus. The Matrix (1999)

"A pure sensation is an abstraction never realized in adult life. Anything which affects our sense organs does also more than that: It arouses processes in the hemispheres which are partly due to the organization of that organ by past experiences, and the results of which in consciousness are described as ideas which sensation suggests. . . . Sensational and reproductive brain processes combined, then, are what give us the content of our perceptions." William James (1892/2001) Psychology. A Briefer Course

From moment to moment, what comprises our conscious experience of the world that surrounds us? The quotation from the text on psychology written by William James in the late 1800s identifies two components of this experience—our sensations and our perceptions. The first component, sensation, can be primarily viewed as arising from the influence of the environment on numerous sensory organs, e.g., tongue, ears, eyes, etc. The second component, perception, derives from complex interactions among numerous neural systems. What James recognized, but which is often not fully appreciated, is that conscious perception of experiences is not just the simple sum of our sensory experiences, rather our sensations are often transformed by the process of perception. During the process of perception people do not merely reconstruct reality, they create it. But the reality they create is also influenced by which stage of

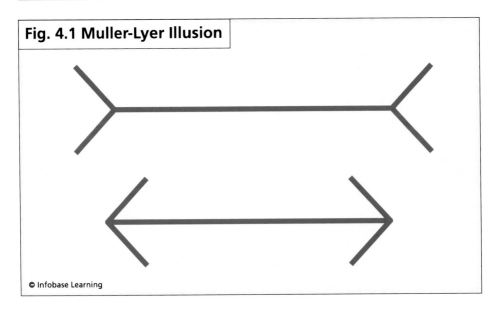

Fig. 4.1 Muller-Lyer Illusion

© Infobase Learning

Which of the two horizontal lines is longer?

development their bodies and brains are passing through and how past inter-actions with the environment have altered them. This is vividly illustrated by numerous perceptual illusions and when the normal processes of perception are distorted or altered by psychotropic drugs, brain injury, or disease. Consider the following classic perceptual visual illusions.

The puzzle in Figure 4.1 is called the Muller-Lyer Illusion. Most people per-ceive the upper horizontal line to be longer than the lower line. In fact, both lines are exactly the same in length. The puzzle in Figure 4.2 is called the Kanizsa Tri-angle. What most people see when looking at this image is two overlapping tri-angles, one pointing upward and the other pointing downward. Actually, there are no uninterrupted triangles in the image—the edges of both triangles are not continuous, however there is a very strong perception that these edges exist.

Although the visual illusions in these two figures are among the most com-mon illusions discussed in introductory psychology courses, our other percep-tual systems are also subject to illusions. Thunberg's Thermal Grill Illusion is an example of a tactile illusion. This illusion requires a willing participant who is asked to place the palm of his or her hand on the metal bars of a grill. The tem-perature of these metal bars can be thermostatically controlled, and the grill is arranged in a manner that alternates warm (40°C) and cool (20°C) bars. Keep in mind that normal skin temperature may range from 30 to 37°C, more or less about what the average temperature across the grill might be. Although neither the cool nor the warm bars would normally be perceived as particularly uncomfortable to the touch, most people who engage in this exercise report the experience as "stinging," "burning," and very painful.

Another dramatic and counterintuitive example of a tactile illusion was recently reported by Valerai Petkova and Henrik Ehrsson of the Karolinska Institute in Sweden. In their study, Petkova and Ehrsson describe a procedure that effectively altered the tactile perceptions of the participants such that they were convinced that one of their arms had been replaced with a rubber prosthetic. Participants in the study were seated at a table with one arm positioned behind a screen and thus out of view (See Figure 4.3). In preparing each participant, the experimenter positioned a rubber arm on the table in front of them and draped a fabric cloth across both the visible real arm and the prosthetic arm so that the prosthetic seemed to occupy the space their hidden arm would normally have occupied if it were extended directly within their view. Next the experimenter simultaneously stroked both the forefinger on the prosthetic hand and on the participant's hand that had been positioned behind the screen. Gradually the participants reported that they were left with a very powerful perception that the prosthetic arm was an extension of their own body and that the tactile sensations they experienced originated from within the prosthetic. By the way, the illusion does not occur

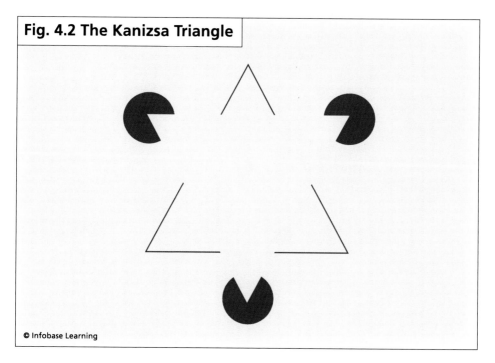

Fig. 4.2 The Kanizsa Triangle

© Infobase Learning

How many triangles do you see?

when a participant is blindfolded; the person must see the rubber arm being touched and must see the prosthetic in a position where his or her own real arm might be.

What can be concluded from these examples of tactile misperceptions? The first thing is that many of our perceptions arise from interactions among multiple features within the same sensory modality (e.g., cold vs. hot tactile stimuli). A second conclusion is that in some instances multiple sensory modalities may contribute to the perception of a unitary perceptual experience (e.g., visual and tactile sensory experiences contribute to the perception that a rubber arm is one's own arm). A third concept revealed here is that perceptions are constructions made by the brain in ways that constitute representations of the sensory world surrounding us. Lastly, representations that the brain constructs may be different from the physical properties of the stimuli that contribute to them. As William James observed, "A pure sensation is an abstraction never realized in adult life."

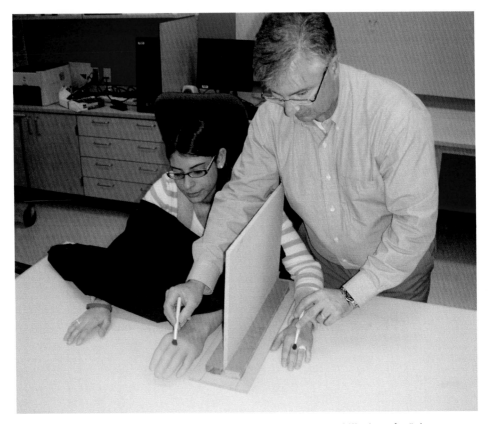

Fig. 4.3 Experimental arrangement employed to elicit the perceptual illusion of a "phantom touch." *(Michael Kerchner)*

Thankfully, our perceptions are accurate enough, so we manage to get by pretty well in the physical world surrounding us. But the ways in which our perceptions may be inaccurate or insufficient approximations of the physical world have fascinated psychologists for centuries, because these inaccuracies and inadequacies provide insights into the neural perceptual processes and the way that the brain reconstructs our experiences. What has been learned has provided the basis for a greater understanding of some rather astounding neurological phenomenon. Three of these intriguing phenomena are described below. **Blindsight** refers to an instance in which someone that is functionally blind as a result of brain injury (not blind due to damage to the eyes). Such individuals report subjectively that they cannot see at all. However, they respond to some visual stimuli, indicating that while there is no conscious awareness of any residual visual perceptual abilities, they can still "see." For example, some patients can reliably catch an object that is tossed to them even though they state that they saw nothing at all. The possibility that they may have sensed an approaching object via another sensory modality (e.g. via hearing or by sensing movement of air as the object approached) can be ruled out because some individuals can reliably detect the apparent movement of images displayed on a computer screen. If they were to view a 3-dimensional movie on a 3-D television, such persons might be startled when objects on the screen appear to move toward them rapidly and unexpectedly. In a similar vein, a video recently posted on the Internet showed an individual with blindsight walking down a narrow hallway, successfully avoiding various objects that cluttered the floor.

What could explain this? As will be apparent as we explore the organization of the human visual system, there are multiple pathways or modules that process different features of our visual perceptual experiences, including color, movement, and object recognition. Long ago, neuroanatomists recognized that specific regions of the cortex play critical roles in processing specific types of sensory stimuli—auditory, visual, tactile, olfactory, and gustatory (taste). These comprise what are regarded as the primary sensory cortices. However, in addition to these primary sensory cortices there are accessory cortical and subcortical regions that also contribute to processing sensory stimuli and our perceptions of them. In cases of blindsight, damage to the primary visual cortex results in cortical blindness. However, some aspects of visual perception that are accomplished by accessory sensory systems that have not been damaged remain relatively unaffected. This may explain why individuals with blindsight report that they are totally blind even though they may retain some aspects of visual perception. At the same time, they are consciously unaware they possess any ability to see. Some may be unable to see light, color, or objects, but may be able to perceive visual movement.

A second unusual neurological phenomenon is prosopagnosia, which is introduced here from a personal and rather universal perspective. I often have difficulty recognizing someone that I've met just once or someone who was a student in one of my classes several years ago. Sometimes I may recognize that a face is somewhat familiar, but I have difficulty recalling the person's name and can't remember where or when or why I have seen this person before. It is likely you have had similar experiences, as they are not at all unusual. Now imagine having the same reaction upon seeing some member of your own family. Or being unable to recognize your own reflection in a mirror. **Prosopagnosia** is a condition in which patients experience great difficulty recognizing faces of people known to them, including in some cases their own reflection. Although prosopagnostic individuals may have excellent visual acuity and may even be able to describe specific facial features of those they are looking at, they are unable to assemble the individual facial features (e.g., hair color, eyes, nose, lips, mouth ears, etc.) into a distinctive whole that characterizes the unique appearance of an individual face. Prosopagnosia can result from stroke, injury, or a degenerative disease frequently affecting a region of the brain called the **fusiform face area** (FFA). However, recent estimates suggest that many more people than expected may have a less severe form of this deficit, one which is called face-blindness or developmental prosopagnosia. Faceblind.org is a Website that has been established by researchers at Harvard University and University College London where you can test yourself to determine if you may have a mild prosopagnosia. Mild prosopagnosia need not be debilitating; in some cases, it can promote interesting achievements. One example is the work of Chuck Close, a very successful artist who has made a career of creating mural-sized artworks depicting the faces of celebrities. These images are often constructed from smaller multicolored patches of canvas that appear as a distinctive facial image only when viewed from a distance.

The deficit experienced in prosopagnosia illustrates what many neuroscientists and philosophers regard as one of the fundamental mysteries of brain function. How are individual sensory elements combined to form a unified perception? How are the distinctive appearance of your father's eyes, hair, lips, ears, cheeks etc., bound together to become a distinctively recognizable face? These questions are part of what psychologists call the **Binding Problem**. As will be discussed at the end of this chapter, the various sensory features that comprise our perceptions are processed in modules that are scattered across different regions of the brain. Yet somehow, this information is combined to form a unitary percept, e.g., the visage of your father and the sound of his voice, or the distinctive taste and texture of a favorite food. While the FFA may be a place where binding of sensory stimuli that comprise facial perceptions occurs, just how this is accomplished is still unclear. According to one theory, this is accomplished through the coordination of synchronous patterns of brain activation in all those distributed brain regions that process the sensory features (sounds, tastes, smells, textures and sights) that comprise our unitary perceptions of people, objects, and places.

Our perceptions of people and objects are not limited to sensory elements alone but to the memories and emotions that are associated with them. Now imagine what people might think if you were to tell them that your mother or father has mysteriously been replaced by an imposter who somehow appeared to be identical to your parents in every respect. Such delusions may occur as a result of significant brain injury or as a result of a neurodegenerative disease. They are part of an exceptionally rare and puzzling condition known as the **Capgras Syndrome.** Psychologist V.S. Ramachandran has proposed an intriguing explanation for such delusions. In essence, Ramachandran argues that our ability to recognize specific individuals derives not only from their physical appearance but also from the emotions that we associate with them. Patients with Capgras syndrome may discern no physical change in the appearance of someone they know extremely well (mother, father, wife, child), but are unable to experience the same emotional attachments that they previously associated with that person. Although these individuals look exactly the same as they always have, the appearance cannot evoke any once-familiar associative emotion. According to Ramachandran, one reason for this may be that the regions of the brain which process emotions have become disconnected from the FFA.

Capgras Syndrome, blindsight, and prosopagnosia illustrate some important perceptual principles of sensation and perceptual processes:

1. Sensory and perceptual processes are distributed among numerous networks within the brain.
2. Within a specific network (e.g., the visual network) there are separate components that process different features of sensory and perceptual experiences.
3. Most perceptions are the combination of representations among multiple sensory systems that have been bound together to form a unitary representation of people, objects, and events we experience.
4. Although one component within a network may be compromised by injury or disease, other components within the same network or other networks can still function normally and may even compensate for the function that has been lost.
5. Injury or disease affecting higher components in the network, those in which perceptual binding occurs, can result in profound perceptual distortions or losses.

The next two chapters explore the organization of these networks one sensory system at a time. Chapter 5 deals with what some consider the minor sensory and perceptual systems; Chapter 6 covers those generally considered to be the major systems.

Further Reading

Carey, B. "Blind, Yet Seeing: The Brain's Subconscious Visual Sense." *New York Times*; December 23, 2008. Available at http://www.nytimes.com/2008/12/23/health/23blin.html. Retrieved November 2011.

Craig, A.D. & Bushnell.M.C. "The Thermal Grill Illusion: Unmasking the Burn of Cold Pain." *Science* 265 (1994): 252–255

Faceblind.org. Available at http://www.faceblind.org/facetests/index.php. Retrieved November 2011.

James, W. *Psychology: The Briefer Course.* Mineola, NY : Dover Publishers, 1892 [2001].

Melzack, R. "Phantom Limbs." *Scientific American* 16 (September 2006): 52–59.

Petkova V.I., and H.H. Ehrsson. "When Right Feels Left: Referral of Touch and Ownership Between the Hands." *PLoS ONE* 4, no. 9 (2009): e6933.

Psychology: The briefer course [1992/1920]. Available at http://www.archive.org/details/psychologybriefe00willuoft. Retrieved November 2011.

Ramachandran,V.S., and D. Rogers-Ramachandran, D. "It's All Done with Mirrors." *Scientific American Mind* 18 (August 2007): 16–18.

TED Talks: VS Ramachandran on Your Mind [Capgras and Phantom Limb]. Available at http://www.ted.com/talks/vilayanur_ramachandran_on_your_mind.html. Retrieved November 2011.

CHAPTER 5

THE "MINOR" SENSES

Suppose for a moment that you were totally impaired in one of your senses. Which sense would it be most debilitating to be without? What would create the greatest impairment in daily functioning? Losing the ability to hear? Losing the ability to see? Which sensory ability would you miss least?

Chances are that you know someone who is deaf or blind. If not personally, then through familiarity with a movie or a book about someone famous who was deaf or blind. It is more than likely that you know the story of Helen Keller, who was both blind and deaf. But consider how much Helen Keller was able to accomplish in her life, even with this double impairment.

Now imagine what it would be like to have no ability to taste something or smell something. What risks might you face because of this? Could you rely on your remaining senses to compensate for not being able to taste or smell? Although it may be that these are minor deficits, consider for a moment how such impairments would affect your health and quality of life. Any sensory or perceptual deficit is challenging, but whether you believe it or not, it may be more difficult to compensate for total loss of the senses of smell and taste than the loss of either vision or hearing.

OLFACTION (SMELL)
Consider the subtle, yet complex, differences between the scent of an orchid, rose, lavender, leather, cedar, pine, rosemary, perfumes, and any other numerous olfactory stimuli that you can readily differentiate from others. You can

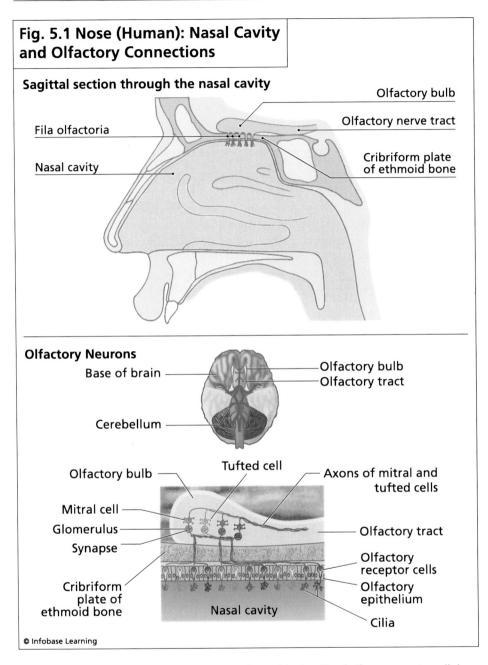

Fig. 5.1 Nose (Human): Nasal Cavity and Olfactory Connections

Sagittal section through the nasal cavity

Olfactory bulb

Olfactory nerve tract

Fila olfactoria

Cribriform plate of ethmoid bone

Nasal cavity

Olfactory Neurons

Base of brain

Olfactory bulb
Olfactory tract

Cerebellum

Tufted cell

Olfactory bulb

Axons of mitral and tufted cells

Mitral cell

Glomerulus

Synapse

Olfactory tract

Olfactory receptor cells

Cribriform plate of ethmoid bone

Nasal cavity

Olfactory epithelium

Cilia

© Infobase Learning

The primary olfactory system. Odor receptors are located in the cilia of olfactory receptor cells in the epithelial tissue lining the upper portion of the nasal cavity and their sensory neural fibers pass through the cribriform plate to synapse directly in the glomeruli of the olfactory bulbs. Within the olfactory bulbs, numerous olfactory fibers synapse within sensory glomeruli with dendrites of olfactory mitral cells. The axons of these mitral cells ultimately form the olfactory nerves that project to pyriform and orbitofrontal lobes of the cortex as well as numerous subcortical nuclei.

probably appreciate why investigators have found it to be a significant challenge to determine the precise mechanisms through which olfactory receptors code for the vast array of olfactory perceptions we experience. Are there a relatively small number of odorant qualities, primary qualities, from which all perceptions arise? If there were such primary qualities of odors, how many must there be to account for the seemingly infinite distinctive scents that we are capable of perceiving?

The cells that are responsive to odorants are located in the sensory mucosal lining along the roof of our nasal passages. These cells communicate directly with the olfactory lobes of the brain, via neural fibers that cross the bony cribriform plate (think of the small holes that are found on a cribbage board), separating the nasal passages from the cranium containing the brain (see Figure 5.1). These fibers synapse with dendrites of **mitral cells** in distinctive globe-like structures called **olfactory glomeruli**. Each glomerulus receives inputs from olfactory receptor cells that are responsive to similar odorant qualities. Therefore, each glomerulus appears to be specialized for processing somewhat unique olfactory stimuli. Relatively simple odorants as well as more complex odorants activate numerous glomeruli. Glomeruli that respond to similar odorants are functionally grouped within separate regions (zones) within the olfactory bulbs. Additionally, output from the glomeruli and the mitral cells is subsequently combined and integrated within the cortical and subcortical components of the olfactory system.

In 2004, Linda Buck and Richard Axel received a Nobel Prize for their contributions to our current understanding of the sensory mechanisms that enable us to be responsive to a vast array of complex odorants. Their work was greatly advanced by the numerous projects to map the mammalian genome. Using the rodent olfactory system as their model system, Buck and Axel identified genes that code for proteins that function as odorant receptors (OR) in the mammalian olfactory system. From their work, and that of other investigators, we now know that there are thousands of OR proteins. These may be subcategorized into as few as four major groups based upon similarities in their amino acid sequences. Each of these functional OR groups contains hundreds of distinct OR, each responding differently to any odorant. Thus, each OR's response to a given odorant is unique, yet most ORs within one of the subgroups will respond in some way to similar odorants. Ultimately the combined responses of a multitude of OR contribute to a unique pattern of neural activation that accounts for our ability to perceive the complex and subtle distinctions between an exceptionally wide range of odors (See Figure 5.2).

One of the interesting facts that has been learned about human ORs is that, although we possess many of the same genes for OR in mice, hundreds of these genes are no longer functional—they do not produce the proteins needed to construct a functional OR. This may be one reason why our olfactory sense may not be as acute as those of other mammals. Perhaps our species' reliance upon visual and auditory senses has come at the costs of our olfactory abilities.

Anosmia refers to a loss of sensory or perceptual abilities in olfaction. There are selective anosmias as well as instances of total anosmia. Because of an inher-

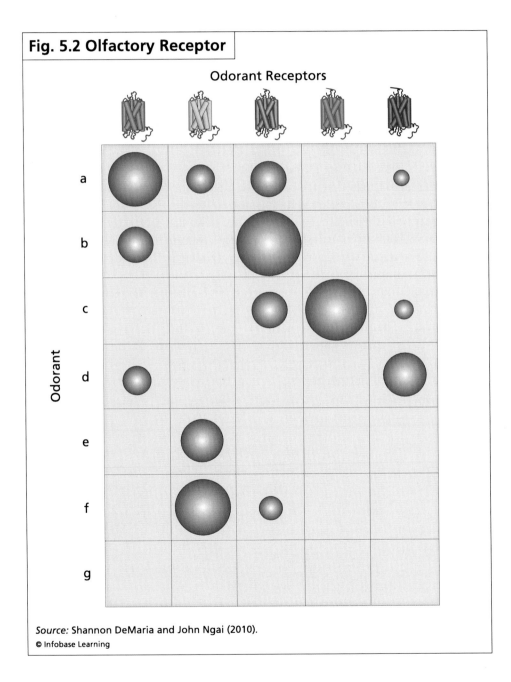

Fig. 5.2 Olfactory Receptor

Source: Shannon DeMaria and John Ngai (2010).

© Infobase Learning

ited variation in olfactory receptors, some percentage (estimates have varied widely from fewer than 2% to as many as 75%) of the population is unable to discern the odor of androsterone (ADT). Those individuals who can smell ADT (an androgen found in urine) describe the odor as musky, unpleasant, or foul. In this instance, such selective anosmia may seem to be an asset rather than a deficit. But consider that the ability to discern the odor of ADT may have been an adaptive behavior among our distant ancestors. Perhaps this may still be the case. Other instances of selective anosmia in humans have been documented for the odor of metabolites of asparagus in urine. These selective anosmias may seem at first as though they would not be detrimental, and perhaps even advantageous. For instance there is evidence that individuals who are initially unable to perceive the odor of ADT can eventually overcome this deficit after repeated exposures to ADT. It also may seem reasonable to conclude that being relatively insensitive to a foul odor would be desirable. All the same, other studies indicate that ADT is capable of exherting subtle effects on mood and behaviors, and investigations have been launched to determine if ADT may be a candidate human **pheromone**; one that compared with males, females may find relatively attractive—or at least less repelant. A pheromone is a chemosignal that is produced by an individual organism, released into the environment and that influences the behavior or physiology of another individual belonging to the same species. Studies that have tried to determine if there are human pheromones have shown that we are remarkably sensitive to some odors and that odors do have the ability to alter our moods and affect behavior, but thus far no odorant that has been proven to function as a pheromone.

Inherited selective olfactory anosmias and hypersomnias are generally caused by genetic variations in specific the olfactory receptors. However, total anosmia is more often the result of mild to moderate traumatic brain injury that damages the pathways connecting the olfactory receptors and the primary olfactory cortex or of neurodegenerative disease (e.g., Parkinson disease or Alzheimer disease). Most of us, however, have experienced only a moderate loss of our sense of smell, something that is likely to occur when you have a very severe cold with nasal congestion.

(opposite page) Perceptual processing of individual odorants is accomplished by integrating the patterns of activity that are elicited from thousand of olfactory receptors (OR). These can be placed within subgroups (represented here by different colors) in which each OR within a subgroup responds to odorants composed of molecules with similar structures and properties. However, the patterns of response that an odorant evokes within and across OR subgroups is uniquely differently. The illustration to the left depicts hypothetical activation of five different OR subgroups to seven different odorants. The larger the circles, the greater the OR response evoked by the odorant. Ultimately distinctive patterns of neural activity can be generated by the unique perceptual characteristics that distinguish one odorant from others.

The other side of the coin is olfactory hypersensitivty (**hyperosmia**), which has been found to occur among some individuals for the odor of isovaleric acid. This selective hyperosmia has been attributed to genetic variants in specific OR genes. Global hyperosmia is extremely rare, but perhaps this is because it is far less debilitating than total anosmia and therefore is not often reported. In general, women appear to be superior in odor discrimination and detection tasks than men; when one sex outperforms the other in odor detection studies it is more common for women to surpass the men. What accounts for this sex difference is not fully understood, although hormonal factors associated with changes across women's reproductive cycle have received the greatest attention from investigators.

To summarize, our ability to perceive subtle variations and distinctive characteristics of odorants is derived from the patterns of activity that are generated by interactions among thousands of OR. Another reason that we are capable of distinguishing subtle differences between very complex odorant qualities is our sense of taste, which also contributes to our olfactory experience.

TASTE

Taste and olfaction are very closely related to one another—most often our perceptions of smell and taste result from interactions between these sensory systems. As you have probably learned from experience, a severe cold that inhibits your sense of smell can also diminish your sense of taste. Moderate loss of taste is called **hypogeusia**, whereas a total loss of the ability to taste is called **ageusia.**

There are five different types of taste qualities and different sensory receptors for each quality: salt, sweet, sour, bitter, and **umami**. You may be wondering what umami tastes like. This quality has been described as "savory," "yummy," or "delicious." L-Glutamate has been found to preferentially stimulate umami receptors. This is one reason why monosodium glutamate (MSG) is added to many foods, and why many foods rich in protein taste better when cooked, specifically because heating can produce greater amounts of L-glutamate. Salt receptors respond most strongly to salts such as sodium chloride. Sweet receptors respond most to sugars, but also to artificial sweeteners such as saccharine. Acidic stimuli preferentially activate sour receptors and bitter stimuli, such as quinine and **propylthiouracil** (PROP).

Receptors for these qualities are located on taste buds that are themselves located on sensory papillae (See Figure 5.3). There are three different types of papillae. Circumvallate papillae are located toward the base of your tongue and possess the greatest density of taste buds. The foliate papillae are located at the sides of your tongue just in front of where the circumvallate papillae are situated. These have fewer taste buds than the circumvallate papillae. The fewest taste buds are found on the fungiform papillae that are distributed across the forward two-thirds of the tongue's surface.

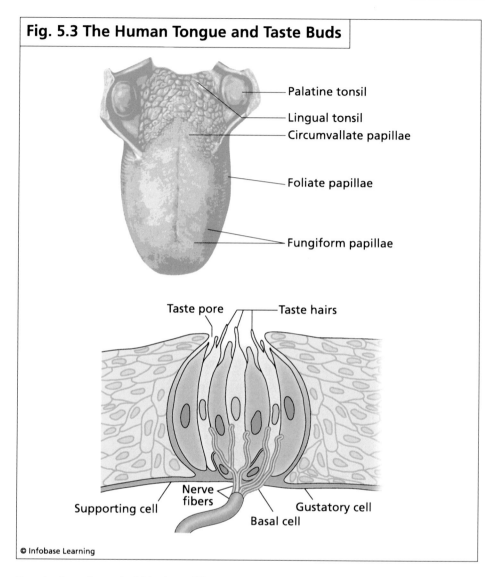

Fig. 5.3 The Human Tongue and Taste Buds

Palatine tonsil

Lingual tonsil

Circumvallate papillae

Foliate papillae

Fungiform papillae

Taste pore

Taste hairs

Supporting cell

Nerve fibers

Gustatory cell

Basal cell

© Infobase Learning

Taste buds are located within three different types of papillae, found in three different regions of the tongue.

The different distribution of the papillae across the tongue and differences in the density of taste buds within each type of papillae suggest that they may serve different functions, for example, coding for different sensory qualities. But it is not at all clear that this is the case. You may have seen maps of the tongue in textbooks, indicating that the receptors for salty, bitter, sweet, and sour qualities were distributed to distinct regions of the tongue (e.g., sweet and salty receptors toward the tip of the tongue; bitter receptors toward the back of the tongue; sour along either side of the middle of the tongue). However, recent research indicates that receptors for these qualities as well as for umami are distributed similarly across the tongue.

How taste is coded by the papillae that comprise taste buds is still debated. According to one model (Figure 5.4a) each sensory nerve that leaves the papillae responds selectively to one of the five qualities. According to the two other models (Figures 5.4b and 5.4c) the activity in each nerve fiber leaving a papilla carries an aggregate of the pattern of activity across the five taste receptors within the cells that comprise the papilla. In one model (Figure 5.4b), each cell contains all five receptors; whereas in another model, the cells within each papilla are specialized for a different taste quality, but multiple cells contribute activity to each nerve leaving the papilla.

The sensory neurons leaving the taste buds enter the brain via several cranial nerves (i.e., the glossopharyngeal nerve, IX; and the facial nerve, VII) and synapse first in several brainstem nuclei and nuclei within the thalamus, before reaching the primary gustatory (taste) cortex—the insula. This is a relatively small region of the cortex that is situated beneath the temporal lobes. Additional outputs from the insula reach other cortical and subcortical structures as

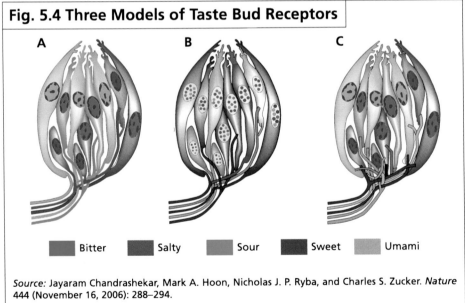

Fig. 5.4 Three Models of Taste Bud Receptors

A   B   C

Bitter   Salty   Sour   Sweet   Umami

Source: Jayaram Chandrashekar, Mark A. Hoon, Nicholas J. P. Ryba, and Charles S. Zucker. *Nature* 444 (November 16, 2006): 288–294.

© Infobase Learning

Three competing theories for the arrangement of various taste receptors with the papillae that comprise each taste bud.

well as receiving reciprocal inputs from these structures. Thus the insula may play an important role in integrating multisensory information culminating in our perception of complex gustatory qualities that arise from the combination of taste, smell, texture, and appearance. Damage to the insula due to stroke has been found to result in deficits in taste perception.

Just as there are individuals who have selective impairments or sensitivities for specific odors resulting from inherited variations in olfactory receptors, some individuals have selective impairments or sensitivities to tastes. Some people, for example, are extremely sensitive to the bitter taste of **propylthiouracil** (PROP). Such supertasters have been studied extensively to determine just what contributes to their enhanced sensitivity to bitterness. Linda M. Bartoshuk, the Director of Human Research at the University of Florida Center for Smell and Taste, has been studying such supertasters for over a decade. Bartoshuk was among the first to show that the number and type of taste receptors that supertasters have on their tongues is different from those that non-tasters (those with PROP hypoguesia) and tasters have. In the United States, roughly 75 percent of Caucasians are able to sense the bitterness of PROP, whereas 25 percent are non-tasters. Of those who are PROP-tasters, just 25 percent are supertasters. Women are also more likely than men to be supertasters. What distinguishes supertasters from the rest of us has to do with the distribution and type of taste receptors on their tongues.

Collectively, the mechanisms of sensory and perceptual processing in the olfactory and gustatory systems share fundamental similarities. There are receptors in each system that are tuned to be responsive to specific qualities derived from the molecular composition and properties of chemical signals. While there are vast differences between the number of sensory receptors within each of the two systems, our perceptions arise from distinctive patterns of activity in the nervous system that arise on multiple levels with our central nervous system. These aspects of sensory and perceptual processing are also replicated in our other senses.

TOUCH AND PAIN

Consider the adjectives that are employed by people to describe the various types of tactile perceptions they experience: tickle, itch, throb, vibrate, etc. In addition there are adjectives that describe the tactile attributes of the objects we encounter in our environment: soft, rough, smooth, cool, hot, heavy, etc. What sensory processes are involved in the construction of such tactile perceptions? Having just reviewed the sensory mechanisms that are involved in the chemical senses you might hazard an educated guess or two. You should at the least know what questions you need to ask and answer to make an educated guess. Are there primary tactile sensory qualities just as there are in olfaction and taste? If so, what may these be? How many different types of sensory receptors are

Fig. 5.5 Receptors in the Skin

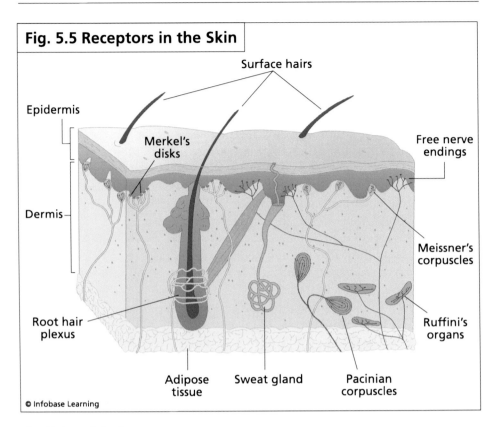

The skin's specialized sensory receptors.

needed to generate the vast range of tactile perceptions that we can conceivably experience? How does each of these primary sensory qualities combine to form a more complex perceptual experience? Where are the signals from multiple tactile receptors integrated to form our perceptual experiences? Do other sensory systems contribute to our tactile perceptions? Let's consider each of these questions.

Your skin is perhaps the largest sensory organ that you possess. Scattered across your body at various depths within your skin are a number of specialized sensory receptors. These include free nerve endings, Merkel's discs, Meissner's corpuscles, Pacinian corpuscles, and Ruffini's endings (see Figure 5.5). Each of these receptors is involved in transducing mechanical stimuli like pressure on the skin or thermal energy applied to the skin into neural activity. Merkel's discs, Messner's and Pacinian corpuscles, and Ruffini's endings are most responsive to mechanical deformation of the skin. Which type of deformation each receptor is most responsive to is determined in part by the receptor's structure, the depth

within the skin where the receptor is typically located, and the response characteristics of the sensory neurons that innervate each type of organ.

The receptor organs found in the deepest layers of the skin, the dermis,
are the Pacinian corpuscles and Ruffini's organs. These are most responsive to
the type of mechanical deformations of the skin that occur from vibration and
stretch, respectively. The sensory neurons that innervate the Pacinian corpuscles are *fast adapting*—meaning that they are very sensitive to rapid mechanical
deformations in the corpuscle that occur when a vibratory stimulus is applied to
the skin. The Ruffini's endings are comparatively *slow adapting*. They respond
with sustained neural activation while the skin is stretched, but are less responsive to abrupt, relatively rapid mechanical deformation of the skin.

The layer of the skin closest to the surface is the epidermis. Meissner's corpuscles and Merkel's discs are specialized tactile organs that are commonly
located in the upper portion of the dermis, the region just below the epidermis.
These receptors are both responsive to touch, but each responds maximally to
specific tactile features of touch. The fast adapting Meissner's corpuscles respond
to the application and removal of a tactile stimulus but are otherwise relatively
inactive. Merkel's discs are relatively slow adapting. As a consequence Merkel's
discs typically respond throughout the time period that a tactile stimulus is in
contact with the surface of the skin. In this way Merkel's discs and Meissner's
corpuscles serve complementary roles in tactile perception of things that we
touch.

Free nerve endings innervate the epidermis and are most responsive to
stimuli that we perceive as painful as well as to thermal stimuli that are applied
to the skin. Free nerve endings also contribute to our perception of itch. Recall
the description of the Thermal Grill Illusion given at the beginning of our discussion of sensory and perceptual systems. In this illusion, cool and warm stimuli that by themselves are not experienced as uncomfortable, will produce a
perception that subjects describe as burning pain when responding to cool and
warm stimuli juxtaposed across alternating segments of the grill. What might
explain this?

There appear to be at least three types of free-nerve ending fibers that contribute to this perceptual illusion. Each is responsive to a different deviation
from the normal temperature of skin (approximately 24°C). One is a fiber that
is most responsive to stimuli that moderately cool our skin. Another is sensitive
to stimuli that warm our skin. And there is also a third fiber (a peripheral **noci-
ceptor**) that is activated by a wide range of stimuli eliciting perceptions of pain
(extreme heat as when we are burned by a lit match or extreme cold as when we
plunge a hand into frigid icy water). All three of these thermoresponsive receptor fibers contribute to an ascending pain pathway (CNC) in the spinal cord and
brain (See Figure 5.6).

When skin temperature does not deviate from normal, the ascending cNC is not activated. However, when alternating surfaces of the skin are simultaneously warmed and cooled as in the thermal grill illusion, the warm fibers negate the ability of the cool fibers to block activity in the cNC pathway. At the same time, activity in the peripheral nociceptors (pNC) is increased. The result is that we experience something perceived as an intense burning sensation although we are not actually being burned.

Based upon the presence of these specialized sensory organs it can be argued that pain, itch, stretch, vibration, and cold/hot constitute the primary

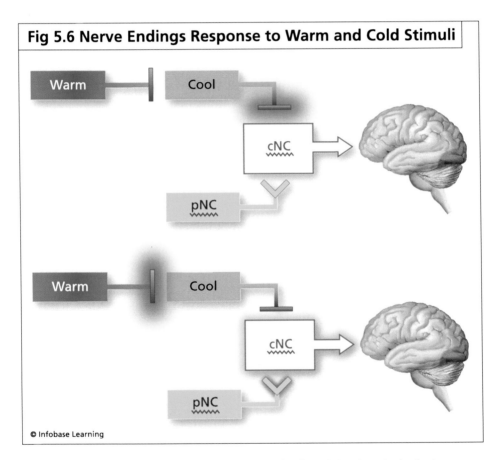

Fig 5.6 Nerve Endings Response to Warm and Cold Stimuli

© Infobase Learning

Central ascending pain (nociception) spinal pathways (cNC) send signals to the brain that are perceived as pain. These are activated by peripheral nociceptive receptors (pNC) that are responsive to a wide range of painful stimuli. Normally, cool stimuli that activate peripheral cool receptors in the skin have an inhibitory influence on such cNC ascending pain signals (*Top*). But when adjacent regions of the skin are warm and cool as in the Thermal Grill Illusion, the signal from peripheral warm receptors inhibit the signal from the peripheral cool receptors, thereby "unmasking" or "amplifying" input from peripheral nociceptors (*Bottom*).

tactile sensory qualities from which all other complex tactile perceptions are constructed. But there is a possibility that there are many more types of receptors that contribute to our tactile sensory perceptions. A recent review of the topic listed as many as ten different types of mechanoreceptors and thermoreceptors in mammalian tissues. Moreover, our tactile perceptions are also influenced by contextual factors such as the social/interpersonal contexts in which we are touched, or even whether the touch is anticipated or not. Have you ever considered why it is difficult to tickle yourself? Experimental evidence indicates that either our intention to act or the self-generated act of tickling itself

Social Exclusion Is Associated with Physical Pain

If you have ever experienced social rejection by your peers or been dumped by someone you have been dating, you may have felt as though you had experienced a physical blow. Obviously you are not the only person who has felt this way, and there is a veritable lexicon of words and phrases that people use to explain the feeling. Among the myriad ways to express the subjective experience social rejection we have "heartache" or "It was as though he/she/they had plunged a knife through my heart!"

Recent research has shown that this is not just a linguistic mechanism but that we may in fact perceive such social rebuffs as physical hurt. In 2003, investigators at the University of California at Los Angeles and Macquarie University in Australia asked participants in a study to engage in a virtual ball-tossing game with other participants via a remote computer connection. All the while that they were engaged in this game, participants' regional brain activity was recorded via functional magnetic resonance imaging (fMRI). Unbeknownst to the participants in the study, they were not playing against other human participants; the game had been set up for each participant to play with virtual players. At some point during the game investigators made the virtual players exclude the participants in the study from the ball-tossing game. The pattern of brain activity observed in victims of this social exclusion was very similar to the pattern of brain activity that occurs following physical injury. Subsequent studies replicated these results and have also found other similarities, including similar patterns accompanying empathic reactions to physical and emotional insults. These studies show a similar pattern of brain activity in people watching someone experience a painful physical blow and people watching someone become a victim of social exclusion. Moreover, it has been shown that acetaminophen, which is commonly used to alleviate physical pain, can also reduce the subjective experience of pain associated with social exclusion as well as reducing activation in brain areas that are normally activated both by social exclusion and painful physical stimuli.

Fig. 5.7 Tactile Sensory Innervation of the Hand

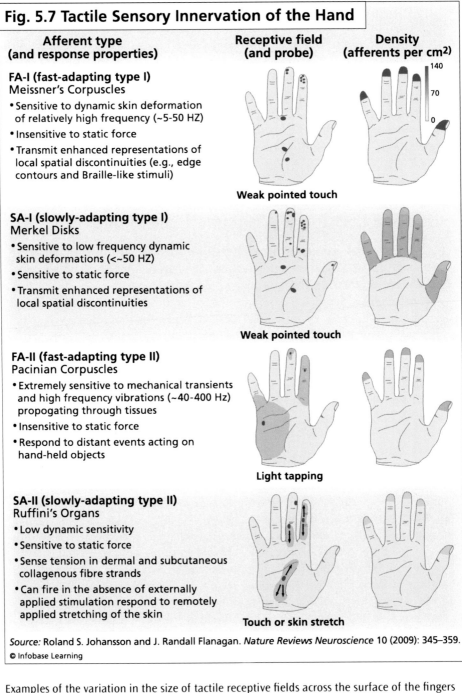

Afferent type (and response properties)	Receptive field (and probe)	Density (afferents per cm²)

FA-I (fast-adapting type I)
Meissner's Corpuscles
- Sensitive to dynamic skin deformation of relatively high frequency (~5-50 HZ)
- Insensitive to static force
- Transmit enhanced representations of local spatial discontinuities (e.g., edge contours and Braille-like stimuli)

Weak pointed touch

SA-I (slowly-adapting type I)
Merkel Disks
- Sensitive to low frequency dynamic skin deformations (<~50 HZ)
- Sensitive to static force
- Transmit enhanced representations of local spatial discontinuities

Weak pointed touch

FA-II (fast-adapting type II)
Pacinian Corpuscles
- Extremely sensitive to mechanical transients and high frequency vibrations (~40-400 Hz) propogating through tissues
- Insensitive to static force
- Respond to distant events acting on hand-held objects

Light tapping

SA-II (slowly-adapting type II)
Ruffini's Organs
- Low dynamic sensitivity
- Sensitive to static force
- Sense tension in dermal and subcutaneous collagenous fibre strands
- Can fire in the absence of externally applied stimulation respond to remotely applied stretching of the skin

Touch or skin stretch

Source: Roland S. Johansson and J. Randall Flanagan. *Nature Reviews Neuroscience* 10 (2009): 345–359.
© Infobase Learning

Examples of the variation in the size of tactile receptive fields across the surface of the fingers and palms.

negates the perception. This illustrates how incoming sensory information may be coded and therefore perceived differently depending upon the influence of descending neural signals originating from other sensory, motor, emotional, and cognitive modules in the brain.

Primary functions of the tactile system are to identify the nature, the source, and the location of things that come into contact with our bodies. To accomplish this with sufficient precision the tactile receptors in our skin are interconnected within specific regions called **receptive fields**. Each tactile receptor responds best to a particular type of tactile stimulus within its own receptive field, and the receptive fields of individual receptors are interlinked within a larger intermediate receptive field. Likewise, slightly overlapping intermediate receptive fields combine their inputs to create tertiary receptive fields. In this manner the entire surface of our bodies is mapped. Ultimately these receptive fields are organized within what are called **dermatomes**.

Figure 5.7 illustrates the variety and distribution of different tactile receptive fields on the palmar surface of the hand. It may not surprise you that the highest density of all types of receptors is localized in the tips of fingers. After all, the tips of your fingers are arguably the most sensitive areas on your hands. Note that different types of receptors have relatively broad receptive fields, whereas other receptor types have relatively small receptive fields. For example, the receptive fields of Meissner's and Merkel's receptors are relatively small. This is what contributes to their relative acuity, i.e. the ability to discriminate two stimuli even though there is little distance between them. In contrast, Pacinian corpuscles, which are responsive to vibration, tend to have the largest receptive fields of all. This is why the source of vibrations may be relatively difficult to localize. Nevertheless, even Pacinian corpuscles in your fingertips have relatively small receptive fields compared to those located elsewhere on your hands. This is why the tips of fingers are so good at discriminating among stimuli with complex and varied textures.

Adjacent tactile receptors combine outputs from their receptive fields to produce intermediate receptive fields. In some instances these are arranged as concentric fields in which stimuli that contact the center elicit increases in neural activity among the tactile receptors that comprise it. Stimulating the surrounding region of the concentric receptive field decreases neural activity among the tactile receptors that comprise it. These are center-on/surround-off receptive fields. There are also center-off/surround-on receptive fields. Shared overlapping outputs from on/off-center and on/off-surround receptive fields combine to produce the dermatomes (see Figure 5.8).

Sensory outputs from the dermatomes enter the spinal cord, where they synapse with interneurons that themselves synapse with sensory neurons on the opposite side of the cord. Fibers from these neurons ascend in the cord and ultimately project to the primary somatosensory cortex located in the parietal lobes. Here the body is mapped onto the cortex in such a way that regions of the body that are most responsive to tactile stimuli are represented by large cortical real estate (See Figure 5.9). Mild localized electrical stimulation of the somatosensory cortex results in the perception of tactile stimulation in the corresponding part of the body. Within the somatosensory homunculus adjacent

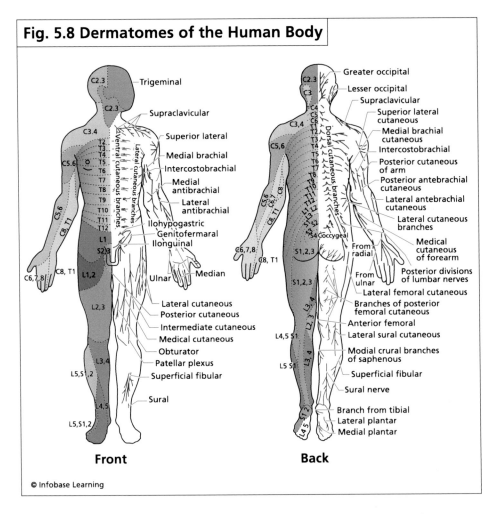

Fig. 5.8 Dermatomes of the Human Body

Front

Back

© Infobase Learning

Dermatomes of the front (*left*) and back (*right*) of the body. In reality the borders between the dermatomes overlap to an extent. Sensory nerve fibers from the tactile receptors in each dermatome enter the spinal cord at different levels; for example, sensory fibers from those dermatomes colored in shades of red-orange enter the spinal cord at the level of cranial vertebrae, whereas those shaded green enter the spinal cord at the level of the 12 thoracic vertebrae.

cortical columns contain neurons that are most responsive to tactile stimuli that correspond with each type of tactile receptor.

The sensory homunculus is dynamic. That is to say, the size of the somatosensory cortex changes to some degree based upon the amount of tactile stimulation that the corresponding region of the body experiences. For example, in professional violinists or in those individuals who play other string instruments the somatosensory area representing the left hand—the hand used to finger the strings—has been found to be slightly larger than the corresponding region that receives sensory input from the right hand. Apparently the increased motor dexterity and sensory acuity required of the left hand relative to the right results

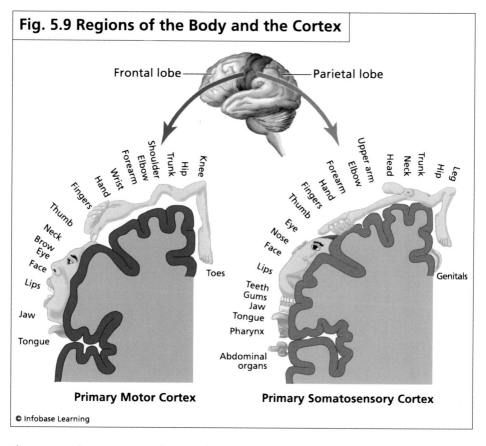

Fig. 5.9 Regions of the Body and the Cortex

Primary Motor Cortex   Primary Somatosensory Cortex

© Infobase Learning

The motor and somatosensory homunculi representative of the primary motor (*left*) and somatosensory cortex (*right*). Note that the regions of the body that require the greatest degree of motor dexterity and tactile sensitivity (e.g., the hands and face) are represented by a greater amount of cortical real estate. These are just two of the regions within the central nervous systems where such homunculi have been identified.

in an expansion of the somatosensory region receiving input from the left hand. The younger the musicians were when they first began their musical training, the greater was the size of the somatosensory cortex representing the left hand. Notably, total de-afferentiation of a limb, such as occurs with the loss of a finger or arm, results in a significant decrease in the size of the corresponding region of the cortex that once received input from the now lost limb. Such plasticity in cortical sensory systems has been suggested as an explanation of the **phantom limb phenomenon.** In some instances individuals who have lost an extremity report that they sometimes perceive that the limb still exists, that they still experience tactile sensations including pain in the missing extremity, and that the limb may feel as though it actually moves on its own. The sudden loss of a finger, hand arm, foot or leg, has been shown to lead to an extensive reorganization of the sensorimotor cortex. As the region that once processed sensory information from the missing limb diminishes in size, the adjacent regions of the somatosensory cortex expand. It is believed that when the parts of the body represented in these expanding regions are stimulated, it may seem as though the source of the sensory stimulation is coming from the lost limb. In effect the remaining region of the somatosensory that had once processed sensations that originated in the missing limb are now receiving mixed signals.

There are three additional complex tactile sensory and perceptual modalities that are rarely are included in introductory courses in psychology. These are **proprioception, kinesthesia,** and **interoception.** Proprioception is the sense that we have of our bodies' position and orientation within the environment. Kinesthesis is a related sensory system that contributes to our perception of our body's movements. The proprioceptive and kinesthetic experiences are derived in part from tactile receptors in our skin and elsewhere deep within our muscles and joints, but also from contributions from other sensory systems, such as vision and balance. There are also sensory receptors deep within the viscera (i.e., our gut). Together, sensations that arise from within the viscera, from our tactile senses, as well as from our proprioceptive and kinesthetic senses, contribute to our overall sense of the state of our body, i.e., interoception. The complex mechanisms that ultimately contribute to our interoceptive perceptions remain to be fully understood and are at the heart of the binding problem that was mentioned at the start of this discussion of sensory and perceptual systems.

Further Reading

Bartoshuk L.M, V.B. Duffy, and I.J. Miller. "PTC/PROP Tasting: Anatomy, Psychophysics, and Sex Effects." *Physiology and Behavior* 56 (1994): 1165– 1171.

Blakemore, S.J., D.M. Wolpert, and C.D. Firth. "Central Cancellation of Self-produced Tickle Sensation." *Nature Neuroscience* 1 (1998): 635–640.

Bremner EA, Mainland JD, Khan RM, Sobel N. "The Prevalence of Androstenone Anosmia. *Chemical Senses, 28*, no. 5 (2003): 423-432.

Chandrashekar, J., M.A. Hoon, N.J.P. Ryba, and C.S. Zuker. "The Receptors and Cells for Mammalian Taste." *Nature* 444 (2006): 288–294.

DeWall, C.N., G. MacDonald, G.D. Webster, C.L. Masten, R.F. Baumeister, C. Powell, D. Combs, D.R. Shurtz, T.F. Stillman, D.M. Tice, and N.I. Eisenberger. "Acetaminophen Reduces Social Pain: Behavioral and Neural Evidence." *Psychological Science* 21, no. 7 (2010): 931–937.

DiMaria, S. and Ngai, J. "The Cell Biology of Smell." *The Journal of Cell Biology* 191, no. 3 (2010): 443–452.

Eisenberger, N.I., M.D. Lieberman, and K.D. Williams. "Does Rejection Hurt? An fMRI Study of Social Exclusion." *Science* 302 (2003): 290–292.

Elbert, T., C. Pantev, C. Wienbruch, B. Rockstroh, and E. Taub. "Increased Cortical Representation of the Fingers of the Left Hand in String Players." *Science* 270, no. 5234 (1995): 305–307.

Johansson, R.S., and J.R. Flanagan. "Coding and Use of Tactile Signals from the Fingertips in Object Manipulation Tasks." *Nature Reviews Neuroscience* 10 (2009): 345-359.

Lumpkin E.A., and M.J. Caterina. "Mechanisms of Sensory Transduction in the Skin." *Nature* 445, no. 7130 (2007): 858–865.

Melzack, R. "Phantom Limbs." *Scientific American* 16 (September 2006): 52–59.

Mori, K., H. Nagao, and Y. Yoshihara. "The Olfactory Bulb: Coding and Processing of Odor Molecule Information." *Science* 286 (1999): 711–715.

The Nobel Prize in Physiology or Medicine 2004: Richard Axel & Linda B. Buck. Availble at http://nobelprize.org/nobel_prizes/medicine/laureates/2004/

NPR: Why 'Supertasters' Can't Get Enough Salt by Allison Aubrey. Available at http://www.npr.org/templates/story/story.php?storyId=127914467. Retrieved November 2011.

Pritchard, T.C., D.A. Macaluso, and P.J. Eslinger. "Taste Perception in Patients with Insular Cortex Lesions." *Behavioral Neuroscience* 113, no. 4 (1999): 663–671.

Ramachandran, V.S., and D. Rogers-Romachandran. "Phantom Limbs and Neural Plasticity." *Archives of Neurology* 57(2000): 317–320.

Schmelz, M. "Itch and Pain." *Neuroscience and Biobehavioral Reviews* 34, no. 2 (2010): 171–176.

Smith, D.V., and R.F. Margolskee. "Making Sense of Taste." *Scientific American* 16 (September 2006): 84–92.

Wysocki CJ, Dorries KM, Beauchamp GK. "Ability to Perceive Androstenone can be Acquired by Ostensibly Anosmic People." *Proceedings of the National Academies of science U S A.* 86, no 20 (1989): 7976-7978.

CHAPTER 6

THE MAJOR SENSES: AUDITION AND VISION

AUDITION (HEARING)

Wherever you may be as you read this, close your eyes. Sit quietly and listen carefully to your surroundings. What do you hear? Can you identify each of the sounds you hear as well as their location? Slowly turn your head to one side and then to the other side. Were you able to identify any sounds you had not previously identified? Were you able to locate the source of some sounds that you previously couldn't place?

Our ability to discriminate different sounds and to pinpoint their location in our environment is something that we often take for granted and often underestimate. To appreciate how finely tuned and sensitive our hearing is, it is illustrative to engage in the exercise above in a variety of settings, for example, outdoors, while riding in a car, listening to a concert, or while lying in your bed at night in the dark.

The two primary features of the sounds that surround us are their amplitude (intensity/loudness) and their frequency (pitch). Amplitude and frequency are the physical properties of sound, whereas intensity/loudness and pitch represent our perception of these properties. The amplitude of a sound is a measure of the magnitude of changes in the pressure caused by sound waves that impinge on our ears. Measures of the amplitude of a sound are expressed in decibels (dB). Table 6.1 compares the amplitude in decibels of some common sounds. Knowing about sound levels is important because noise-induced hearing loss is a major occupational hazard in numerous professions. Hearing loss is most likely in professions where workers are likely to encounter sounds over 100 dB, but extended exposure to noises between 85 and 95 dB can also cause appreciable loss of hearing. Standards set by the National Institute on Occupational Safety and Health (NIOSH) indicate that for every 3 dB above 85 dB, the permissible time limits of exposure are cut in half.

In everyday life, portable music players at higher volume settings can generate amplitudes in headphones that easily exceed 85 dB. This has generated concern about the prevalence of hearing loss among regular users of portable music players. At 100 dB, the chances of sustaining hearing deficits are elevated after 15 minutes of listening; at 110 dB damaging effects may be detectable within just 2 minutes. Table 6.1 also illustrates the sound levels of different sources that people may encounter in everyday life and the level at which sounds become painful.

Loudness is determined by the physical intensity of a sound; pitch is determined by the frequency of the sound waves. The higher the frequency, the higher is the pitch. The frequency of a sound is measured in hertz (Hz). The

TABLE 6.1
The Comparative Amplitude of Common Sounds

Sound Source	Amplitude (dB) *
Breathing	10 dB
Whisper	20 dB
Rainfall	50 dB
Normal conversation	60–70 dB
Garbage Disopsal/Dishwasher	80 dB
Subway Train	95 dB
Motorcycle	100 dB
Average Human Pain Threshold	100 dB
Loud Rock Concert	108–115 dB

*Note:** The amplitude of the noise generated by each source in this table depends upon the distance from the source as well as upon the frequencies that comprise noise. The decibel scale is also logarithmic; changes in intensity are exponential, e.g., a whisper is 10 times louder than breathing.

Human Echolocation

Take a second to recall the classic image of a blind person navigating through pedestrian traffic with the aid of a red-tipped white walking cane. Perhaps, like me, you assumed that the cane's function was to feel out obstacles the blind person might otherwise stumble upon. The primary perceptual process in this case would be dependent exclusively on the tactile sense of the environment. However, consider why blind people frequently use the cane to strike or tap the surface of the ground; they do not merely wave it about in the air in front of them. The tapping is a means of echolocation. The sound of the tapping is reflective of the surrounding surfaces. Not only can the echo be used to help judge the distance of the person from obstructions, but the character of the returning sound is altered by the nature of the surface from which it is reflected. Glass, steel, plastic, and cloth all produce distinctly different echoes, thereby helping the person to discern the different character of each object's surface. With practice, a sighted person can also become adept at using echolocation. You can try this yourself with a blindfold, a cane, and a friend to help guide you while you practice. In fact, sighted individuals probably use echolocation to help them identify the direction of origin for many sounds in the environment; the difference is that they are not conscious that they are doing so.

A remarkable example of the use of echolocation by the blind was featured in a recent segment of the National Public Radio (NPR) program All Things Considered. The story features the remarkable abilities of Daniel Kish, founder of World Access for the Blind (http://www.worldaccessfortheblind.org). Blind since he was very young, Kish has honed his ability to utilize echolocation to navigate in his environment whether walking or even while riding a bike. He has even led groups of blind cyclists on mountain biking excursions along unfamiliar paths.

human auditory system is capable of discerning frequencies between 20 Hz and 20 kHz (cycles per second). By comparison, bats are capable generating and discerning ultrasounds that are many times higher in frequency than 20 kHz. Many rodents communicate with each other using ultrasonic vocalizations. For example, infant mice and rats produce ultrasonic distress vocalizations when separated from their littermates and their dam. Some insects can generate ultrasounds as countermeasures used to defeat echolocation by bats. The size of the animal is not a good predictor of whether it may utilize ultrasounds to help it navigate or identify potential prey. Some toothed cetaceans (e.g., orcas, sperm whales, and dolphins) produce ultrasonic clicks to locate, and potentially incapacitate, squid they prey upon. Although humans cannot hear ultrasounds, we are capable of echolocation using those sounds we can discern.

Fig. 6.1 The Middle and Inner Ear

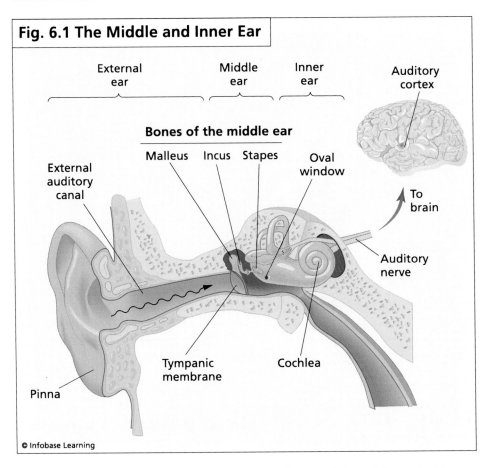

The middle and inner ear consists of the tympanic membrane and three of the smallest bones in your body: the malleus (hammer), incus (anvil), and stapes (stirrup). These small bones transfer deformations in the tympanic membrane to the cochlea.

At the other end of the continuum, elephants and whales have been found to communicate via exceptionally low frequencies, infrasounds, well below 20 Hz. A wide variety of animals, including insects, amphibians, fish, and birds, are also able to communicate via infrasonic calls. Although such infrasounds are not easily discernable as sounds by humans, people may be able to feel them, and there is evidence that prolonged exposure to such frequencies as well as brief exposure to high amplitude infrasound generated by explosions can compromise hearing and contribute to other adverse physical symptoms.

The initial stages of auditory sensory and perceptual processing are similar to those of the tactile senses in that they rely chiefly upon mechanoreceptors.

Just as tactile receptors in the skin are responsive to various types of physical deformation of the skin, the auditory system is specialized for transducing the mechanical deformation of the eardrum (tympanic membrane) that occurs when sound waves strike our ears (Figure 6.1). Ultimately this mechanical deformation is conveyed via the ossicles, three small bones (malleus, incus & stapes) of the middle ear to the inner ear, i.e., the cochlea (Figure 6.2). The cochlea contains the receptors that ultimately generate neural activity in the auditory system.

Cochlear auditory receptors are components of the **Organ of Corti (OC).** The OC spans the length of the cochlea's interior and consists of the tectorial membrane, the basilar membrane, and the primary auditory receptors called hair cells. There are three rows of outer hair cells and one row of inner hair cells. The outer hair cells rest upon supporting cells that line the basilar membrane. Bundles of steriocilia at the tips of the hair cells are in contact with the tectorial membrane (See Figure 6.3).

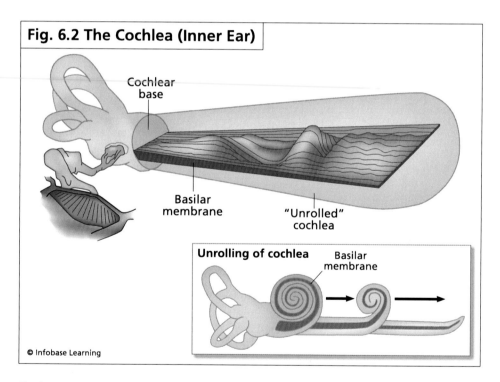

Fig. 6.2 The Cochlea (Inner Ear)

Cochlear base

Basilar membrane

"Unrolled" cochlea

Unrolling of cochlea   Basilar membrane

© Infobase Learning

The inner ear, or cochlea, contains the Organ of Corti—our primary auditory sensory organ. The cochlea contains three fluid-filled chambers and the basilar membrane. Sounds of different frequencies cause deformations along specific regions of the basilar membrane.

When sounds strike the tympanic membrane, the stirrup begins to move in and out of the cochlea's oval window. This movement establishes pressure waves in the fluid within the OC, and these pressure waves deform the

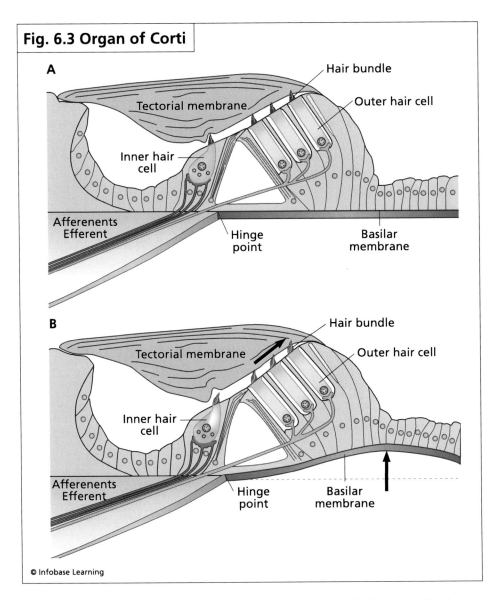

Fig. 6.3 Organ of Corti

A

Hair bundle

Tectorial membrane

Outer hair cell

Inner hair cell

Afferents
Efferent

Hinge point

Basilar membrane

B

Hair bundle

Tectorial membrane

Outer hair cell

Inner hair cell

Afferents
Efferent

Hinge point

Basilar membrane

© Infobase Learning

There are three rows of outer hair cells and one row of inner hair cells. The stereocilia of the inner and outer hair cells are in contact with the tectorial membrane. Deformations of the basilar membrane exert a shearing force in the steriocilia as the hair cells shift relative to the tectorial membrane. In this way, pure tones of a specific frequency activate specific sets of hair cells along the length of the basilar membrane.

basilar membrane. High frequency tones cause deformations in the basilar membrane nearest to the oval window. Low frequency tones cause deformations along portions of the basilar membrane furthest from the oval widow, toward the tip (apex) of the cochlea. Information about the frequency of a sound is coded spatially within the cochlea. High frequency deformations in the basilar membrane cause the stereocilia of the outer hair cells located above the corresponding region of the basilar membrane to bend (shear) ever so slightly, because the tips of their stereocilia are fixed in the tectorial membrane. Low frequency tones stimulate outer hair cells closer to the apex of the basilar membrane. Such mechanical shearing forces stimulate a subset of outer hair cells thereby generating a neural impulse in a corresponding subset of neural fibers within the auditory nerve (cranial nerve VII). Each subset of hair cells responds most strongly to sounds within a specific range of frequency. Thus the frequency of a tone is coded spatially within the cochlea.

How is amplitude of a sound coded? The louder a tone is the greater the amplitude of the deformations in the basilar membrane and the greater the number of hair cells that are stimulated. Furthermore, as this happens, hair cells that normally would not be activated because the frequency of the tone lies beyond the range of frequencies they respond to also begin to be excited. The louder the sound, the greater the number of hair cells that fire across a broad range of frequencies and the greater the overall neural activity in the auditory nerve.

Perhaps you now have insights into why brief exposures to extremely loud sounds or prolonged exposures to moderately loud sounds (between 85 and 100 dB) can result in hearing loss. If the amplitude of a sound is very high, it can result in extremely large deformations of the basilar membrane and excessive shearing forces that can damage the stereocilia of the hair cells. Once damaged beyond repair, the stereocilia cannot be replaced. Such hearing loss is a type of sensorineural deafness (i.e., deafness resulting from disease or damage of the cochlea or auditory nerve). Some antibiotics as well as over-the-counter inflammatory medications and chemotherapy drugs also have been found to cause toxic damage to hair cells, which in some instances have resulted in sensorineural deafness.

The centrally projecting fibers that constitute the auditory nerve leave the cochlea and synapse within the brain stem in the cochlear nucleus on the same side of the head. Fibers leaving the cochlear nucleus on one side synapse within the superior olivary nuclei (SON) on either side of the brain stem. It is at this level that information from both ears may be compared for the first time. (You will read more about the SON when we consider how we localize the source of a sound.) Next, a mix of auditory fibers from the left and right ears project first to the inferior colliculus, then to the medial geniculate nucleus of the thalamus, and ultimately to the primary auditory cortex. The primary auditory cortex is located along the upper margin of the temporal lobe in each cerebral hemisphere. Based upon work with non-human primates as well as with functional imaging of the human brain, it appears that there are dedicated regions within the auditory cortex that are arranged in rows or stripes containing neurons that respond best to tones within a specific range of frequencies and amplitudes (See Figure 6.4). Within each frequency-selective stripe of cortical neurons there are alternating segments that contain neurons that respond best to inputs from both ears (binaural cells) or from either the left or the right ear (monaural cells). The spatial tonotopic representation of various frequencies along the length of the cochlea, high frequencies stimulating hair cells closest to the base of the cochlea and lower frequencies stimulating hair cells closer to the apex, is

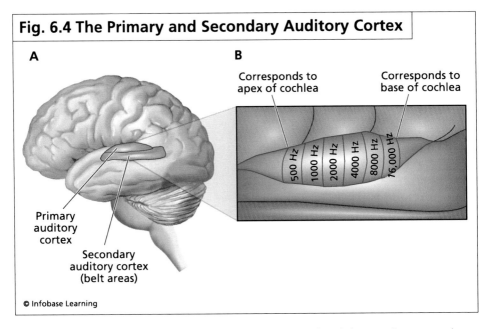

Fig. 6.4 The Primary and Secondary Auditory Cortex

A

B

Corresponds to apex of cochlea

Corresponds to base of cochlea

500 Hz 1000 Hz 2000 Hz 4000 Hz 8000 Hz 16,000 Hz

Primary auditory cortex

Secondary auditory cortex (belt areas)

© Infobase Learning

(A) The primary auditory cortex is located along the inner border of the superior temporal lobe in each hemisphere. Neurons within the auditory cortex are most responsive to sounds of a particular frequency and amplitude. (B) In many non-human primates the spatial (tonotopic) representation of frequency-selective receptors in the cochlea is also maintained in the primary cortex. Although not depicted, in humans it appears that adjacent frequency stripes are tonotopic mirror images of each other. Within each frequency stripe are alternating regions containing monaurally and binaurally responsive neurons. The temporal lobes also contain a secondary (accessory) auditory cortex that is adjacent to the primary auditory cortex. Cells in the accessory auditory cortex appear to be selectively responsive to more complex auditory stimuli.

preserved in the primary auditory cortex. In summary, neurons in the primary auditory cortex that are selectively responsive to similar frequency, intensity, and location are grouped together in a complex yet systematized pattern.

VISION

Before discussing the visual sensory and perceptual systems, it may be helpful to examine some of the common aspects of the systems reviewed thus far.

- Every sensory system has distinct receptors, each tuned to respond most to specific features of sensory stimuli. Such receptors can be considered feature detectors.
- As in the tactile system, feature detectors may have distinct receptive fields—regions on or around our bodies where they are responsive to sensory stimuli.
- The output from these primary feature detectors may be combined at subsequent stages within the sensory systems to create more complex features.
- At the highest levels of sensory processing, complex features bind with one another to create our perceptual experiences.

All of these points are reflected in the sensory and perceptual processes that comprise our vision system, starting with sensory receptors. **Visual photoreceptors** are located within the **retina**; the thin sensory membrane at the rear of each eye. The lens at the front of each eye focuses the light comprising each visual image on the retina.

Light must first pass through several other layers of cells within the retina before reaching the photoreceptors. These are the **ganglion cell** and **bipolar cell** layers. **Amacrine cells** and **horizontal cells** are also found at the juncture between the ganglion and bipolar cell layers and the bipolar and photoreceptor layers, respectively. Recordings from the ganglion cell layer indicate that each ganglion cell responds to stimuli that lie within a specific region of the visual field. This region is the **receptive field** of the cell.

There are two broad categories of visual photoreceptors: the **rods** and the **cones**. As the names suggest, rod cells are rod shaped, whereas cone cells have a distinctive conical shape. The rods are principally responsive under conditions in which levels of light are low (i.e., our **scotopic vision**), whereas the cones are principally responsive during conditions where light levels are high (i.e., our **photopic vision**). You may notice that your ability to distinguish differences in the color (hue) of various objects is poor in low-light conditions (scoptopic conditions). This is because rods respond relatively equally to all wavelengths of light; they do not discriminate well between color variations. In contrast, there are three distinctive types of cones, and each is maximally responsive to light within a specific range of wavelength. Thus when light levels are high (photopic conditions), cones make it possible and easier for you to discern differences in the color features of objects in your environment.

The key differences between rods and cones are not primarily the result of differences in their shapes, but the result of differences in the light sensitive **photo pigments** contained within their respective cell walls. These visual photo pigments are called opsins. Rhodopsin is found within the rods, whereas each cone contains one of three different opsins, and each of these is responsive to light within a specific range of wavelengths. Because there are three distinct opsins in the cones of the human retina, humans have trichromatic color vision. Most other mammals have only two distinct retinal opsins and therefore have dichromatic color vision. According to the **trichromatic**

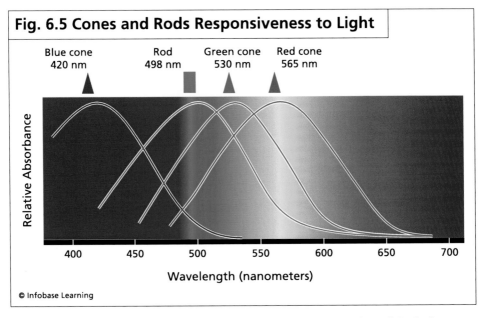

Fig. 6.5 Cones and Rods Responsiveness to Light

A summary of the response sensitivities of the three types of cones and the rods in the human retina. Peak sensitivity of the cones responsive to relatively short wavelengths (S-cones) corresponds with the hue we perceive as blue (420 nm). Peak sensitivities for cones responsive to medium wavelengths (M-cones) correspond with the hue we perceive as green (495 nm). Although the cones that are most responsive to longest wavelengths of light are actually most responsive to yellow (560 nm), they also respond to hues extending the furthest into the red section of the color spectrum. Note that although the peak sensitivity of the rods is to bluish-green light, they function only in dim light.

hypothesis of color vision our ability to discern different hues is enabled by blue-sensitive, green-sensitive, and red-sensitive visual receptors. This theory is consistent with the what we know about cones and their three types of opsins, one of which is most responsive to relatively short (blue) wavelengths, another to medium (green) wavelengths, and the third to longer (red) wavelengths.

However, simply combining the inputs of these three color-responsive cones does not fully account for human ability to discern subtle differences in hues across our full range of color vision. To address this phenomenon, an **opponent-process hypothesis** has been proposed. According to this hypothesis cells within the retina are excited or inhibited by opposing hues; blue-yellow, green-red, and black-white. There is support for this theory as well. Recall that the retina contains a layer of ganglion cells. Evidence indicates that these cells are either excited or inhibited in a fashion that is consistent with the opponent-process hypothesis. Thus an adequate explanation for human color vision must incorporate aspects of both hypotheses for color vision. The initial process of color vision in the retina is likely to be a two-stage process: first a trichromatic process, in which the cones are activated, followed by an opponent process in which they then activate, or de-activate, the ganglion cells.

The two-stage process of visual color perception described above is just one of the initial forms of visual information processes that occur within the retina. Further perceptual processing occurs in subsequent stages along both primary and secondary visual systems within the brain. The pathways that comprise the primary visual system are depicted in Figure 6.6. Fibers from retinal ganglion cells in each eye join to form the left and right optic nerves. Some of the fibers from the optic nerve of each eye cross within the optic chiasm. As a result, visual stimuli in your left visual field are processed in the right cerebral hemisphere, whereas visual stimuli in your right visual field are processed in the left cerebral hemisphere.

The first major processing point for visual information in the primary visual system occurs in the **lateral geniculate nucleus** (LGN) of the thalamus. Within the LGN are six distinct layers of cells. Cells in each of these six layers are responsive to different visual features. Some LGN cells that are similar to ganglion cells in the retina are responsive to color with opponent center-surround receptive fields. These cells occupy the four outermost layers of the LGN, and comprise the **parvocellular** (small cell) component of the LGN. The two innermost cell layers within the LGN contain cells that are much larger and comprise the **magnocellular** (large cell) component of the LGN. These large cells are relatively unresponsive to light of a specific color but are responsive to movement across the visual fields. Although each layer of the LGN receives input from either the left or right eye, the visual response they produce is contralateral: The right LGN processes visual stimuli within the left visual field of each eye; the left LGN processes visual stimuli within

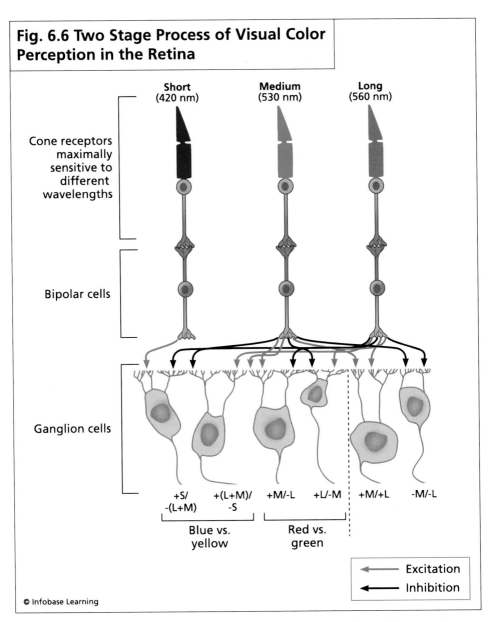

Fig. 6.6 Two Stage Process of Visual Color Perception in the Retina

Short (420 nm)   Medium (530 nm)   Long (560 nm)

Cone receptors maximally sensitive to different wavelengths

Bipolar cells

Ganglion cells

+S/ -(L+M)   +(L+M)/ -S   +M/-L   +L/-M   +M/+L   -M/-L

Blue vs. yellow   Red vs. green

Excitation
Inhibition

© Infobase Learning

A schematic illustration of the two-stage process of visual color perception within the retina. Note that ganglion cells receive both excitatory and inhibitory inputs from pairs of cones with spectral sensitivities that peak at "opposing" wavelengths.

the right visual field of each eye. Just like the ganglion cells in the retina, each LGN cell responds to visual stimuli within its own receptive field.

The receptive fields of LGN cells consist of concentric circular center-surround regions (see Figure 6.8). Some LGN cells are activated when light illuminates the center regions of the receptive field (center-on cells), while others are maximally responsive only when the outermost region of their receptive field is illuminated (on-surround cells). There are also off-center and off-surround

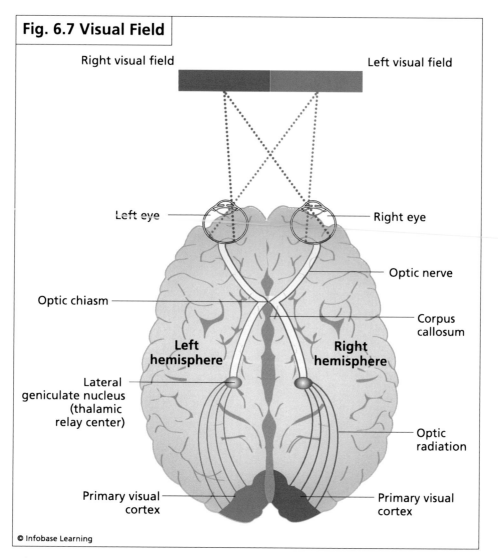

Fig. 6.7 Visual Field

Right visual field

Left visual field

Left eye

Right eye

Optic nerve

Optic chiasm

Corpus callosum

Left hemisphere

Right hemisphere

Lateral geniculate nucleus (thalamic relay center)

Optic radiation

Primary visual cortex

Primary visual cortex

© Infobase Learning

Schematic representation of the primary visual pathways. Note that stimuli in the left visual field are processed within the primary visual pathways of the right hemisphere, whereas the left hemisphere processes stimuli originating from within the right visual field.

LGN cells that are inhibited when these respective regions of their receptive fields are illuminated.

Consider what your vision would be like if this were the sum total of visual processing occurring within the visual system. You might be able to tell when certain regions of your visual field were illuminated by light and you might be able to discern the color of the light as well as movement, but not much else. This is where additional components and processes of the complex visual system come in.

Fibers leaving the left and right LGN form the **optic radiations** within their respective hemisphere and ultimately end up in the **primary visual cortex**. Cells in the primary visual cortex are responsive to much more varied and complex visual features than are cells with the LGN. The primary visual cortex contains cells that have receptive fields very similar to LGN cells, the cortex also contains cells that are responsive to specific visual features. Some cortical cells are maximally responsive to lines, bars, or edges of particular

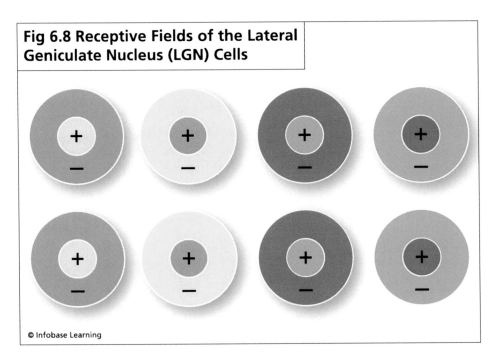

Fig 6.8 Receptive Fields of the Lateral Geniculate Nucleus (LGN) Cells

© Infobase Learning

Representations of opponent center-surround receptive fields of retinal ganglion cells and cells in the lateral geniculate nucleus (LGN) of the thalamus. Whether light that is within the center activates (+) or inhibits (-) the cell depends upon where in the receptive field the illumination occurs. LGN cells within the magnocellular pathway are relatively non-responsive to color. Although LGN cells that comprise the parvocellullar pathway have comparatively smaller receptive fields, they are responsive to color. Input from either the left or right eyes is represented in separate cell layers within the LGN.

width and orientation. These simple visual cortical cells function as edge or line feature detectors. They are arranged in columns perpendicular to the surface of the cortex. All the simple cells found within the same column are selectively

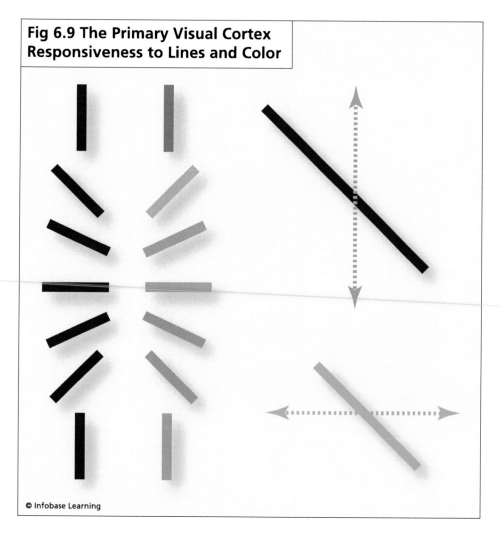

Fig 6.9 The Primary Visual Cortex Responsiveness to Lines and Color

© Infobase Learning

Some cells in the primary visual cortex (V1) have receptive fields that function as line or edge detectors. Some of these edge detectors respond best to a line of a particular orientation (vertical, horizontal, etc.) and/or color. Other V1 cells are more selective feature detectors. These are most responsive to lines of a particular orientation, color, and length, but to elicit a response from these cells, the line must also be moving within the receptive field of the cell in a specific direction. Bi-ocular V1 cells receive input from both the left and right eyes and contribute to our perception of depth (stereopsis). At subsequent levels of processing in accessory visual cortices, cells are most responsive to more complex visual features (e.g., complex forms, objects, faces, scenes, or places).

activated by a line or edge of the similar orientation. Adjacent columns contain simple cells that respond to a line of slightly different orientation, sequentially spanning 360-degrees of rotation. Other cells, the complex visual cortical cells, also respond to lines of a particular orientation and width within their receptive field, but only if these lines move in a specific direction within the receptive field. In addition to orientation columns there are also ocular-dominance columns with cells that are responsive primarily to inputs received from either the left or right eye. There are also orientation columns that are selectively activated by lines of a particular color and other cells that are selectively responsive to high-contrast and low-contrast features.

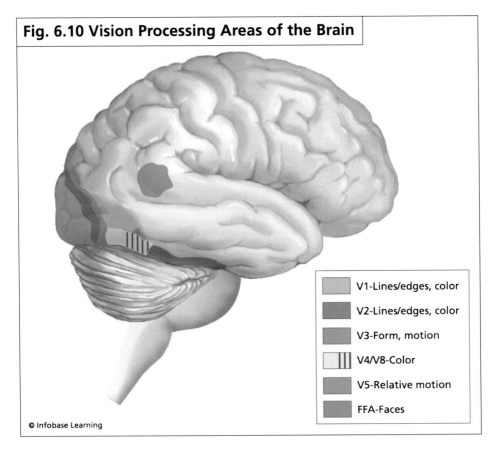

Fig. 6.10 Vision Processing Areas of the Brain

V1-Lines/edges, color
V2-Lines/edges, color
V3-Form, motion
V4/V8-Color
V5-Relative motion
FFA-Faces

© Infobase Learning

An illustration indicating the approximate location of the primary visual cortex (V1) and select accessory visual cortices (V2, V3, V4, V5, V8) and the Fusiform face area (FFA). Note that the largest portions of V1,V2, and V3 are along the midline that separates the left and right occipital lobes. V4/V8 and FFA occupy an extensive region along the bottom of the temporal lobes.

This increasing degree of sophistication in feature detection and analysis stems from the combined interaction of multiple cells functioning to detect various features within multiple parallel visual pathways. Some of this processing takes place outside the primary visual cortex in accessory visual regions of the cortex. There are at least four of these accessory visual cortices (see Figure 6.10). The primary visual area is usually identified as V1 and these other areas as V2, V3, V4, and V5, etc. Areas V1 and V2 contain cells with very similar response properties to those we have discussed to this point. The precise role of cells within V3 is uncertain. Some research suggests that the upper (dorsal) and lower (ventral) components of V3 have slightly different specializations as feature detectors. However, the majority of inputs to V3 appear to originate within the magnocellular components of the LGN and therefore, V3 cells are responsive to movement and form. Inputs to V4 originate primarily from parvocellular components of the LGN and are most responsive to forms and color. Recent research suggests that another accessory visual region of the cortex, designated V8 also appears to participate primarily in processing color.

The emerging pattern of organization among the visual cortices indicates that there may be two major parallel perceptual systems for processing visual information (see Figure 6.11). Projections from one system travel along the bottom (ventral) surface of the temporal lobes. Projections from the other system travel toward the upper (dorsal) surface of the brain through the parietal lobes. It has been proposed that the components of the ventral and dorsal pathways function primarily to construct our visual perceptions of complex objects (the "what") and their location/movement in the environment (the "where"), respectively.

Researchers have identified areas along the ventral stream that appear to be selectively activated by human bodies and body parts (hands, feet, arms, etc.). Other investigators have presented evidence that some cells within the ventral stream are selectively activated by images of things that belong to specific categories of inanimate objects (e.g., tools, chairs). One region within the ventral stream that has been extensively studied is the **fusiform face area (FFA)** located on the bottom of the temporal lobes. As the name suggest, cells here are not just selectively responsive to specific facial features but to the distinctive arrangement of these features that together comprise a facial image. Other primates as well as other mammals (such as sheep) have cortical regions in their brains that are selectively activated by species-specific facial stimuli. Damage to this region due to disease or stroke can result in "face blindness" or prosopagnosia (described in some detail in Chapter 4). .

One of the accessory visual cortices within the dorsal "where" stream is a region called V5. Cells in V5 are specialized for detection and analysis of forms

(continues on page 92)

Achromatopsia

Cold hearted orb that rules the night,
Removes the colours from our sight.
Red is grey and yellow white.
But we decide which is right.
And which is an illusion?

—*From "Late Lament" by the Moody Blues;*
Days of Future Past *(1967)*

Normal photopic trichromatic color vision is dependent upon the presence of the three types of cones (blue, green, and red). In dim light, as during a moonlit night, color perception is degraded because our scotopic vision is largely mediated by rods. Photopic color vision deficiencies occur when one or more of the cones is missing or non-functional. Most forms of color deficiencies are genetic, often X-linked. This means the gene that results in the loss of one or more of the cones is located on the X-chromosome. Such X-linked congenital color deficiencies are most common among males because males have just one X-chromosome. One of the most common forms of color deficiencies results in difficulty distinguishing between red and green (red-green "color blindness"). Individuals who cannot correctly identify the numerals within the circular pattern of colored blotches that comprise the test image from the Ishihara color plate below lack either the red (long-wavelength) or green (medium-wavelength) cones. In a very rare X-linked form of color blindness both red and green cones are absent, a condition called blue-cone monochromatism. And in exceptional instances of congenital color deficiency all three types of cones are absent, leaving only the rods, and resulting in total color blindness or achromatopsia (rod monochromatism). In contrast to the X-linked conditions, congenital achromatopsia is an autosomal recessive disorder. The genes that cause achomatopsia are not on either the X or Y chromosomes, and both parents must contribute a copy of the anomalous gene to their child. So males and females are equally susceptible.

In his book, *The Island of the Colorblind,* neurologist Oliver Sacks interviews Knut Nordby, an achromatopic who is also a vision researcher. Sacks describes their travels to a small atoll in the middle of the Pacific Ocean on which a high proportion of the inhabitants have congenital achromatopsia. An excellent Internet source with a video documentary of their visit to Pinglap, and more information regarding the various types of congenital achromatopsia, may be found at http://www.achromatopsia.info.

All instances of congenital color deficiency are caused by genetic anomalies that affect the function of cones. Cases of acquired (cerebral) achromatopsia are quite rare and result from stroke, disease, or traumatic brain injury that damages the accessory visual cortical regions that process color, e.g., V4. This illustrates that the brain, not the eyes, is ultimately where colors are seen. In *An Anthropologist on Mars*, Oliver Sacks describes the case of "Jonathan I," a painter who was forced to adapt to being totally colorblind after sustaining a mild traumatic brain injury in an automobile accident. The injury had a profound influence not only on his art but also on the overall quality of his perceptual experiences. As Sacks describes, "It was not just that colors were missing, but that what he did see had a distasteful, 'dirty' look' . . . that people's flesh appeared 'an abhorrent grey,' and that Jonathan I found foods disgusting due to their greyish, dead appearance and had to close his eyes to eat." Having never perceived the world in color, congenital achromats do not experience the absence of color in such deeply disturbing ways.

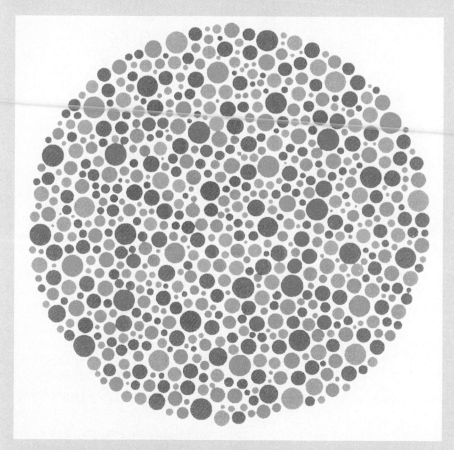

Ishihara color plates are used to assess whether someone is color blind and, if so, the specific nature of the color deficiency. *(Wikipedia)*

(continued from page 89)

and their relative movement. The region is most responsive to features in the environment that occur where movement of adjacent elements in the visual field appear to be disparate: kinetic-boundary perception. To get a sense for where these boundaries occur, look around whatever environment you happen to be in at the moment. Find some stationary objects and focus on them while you move your head from side to side. As you do this you may recognize that objects in the background appear to move in opposition to objects in the foreground

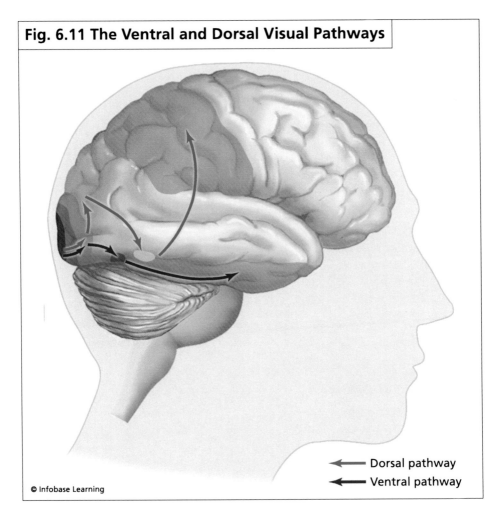

Fig. 6.11 The Ventral and Dorsal Visual Pathways

Dorsal pathway

Ventral pathway

© Infobase Learning

An illustration of the ventral and dorsal components' perceptual streams. It has been suggested that these streams comprise the parallel systems for processing visual information regarding "what" (purple arrows) and "where" (green arrows).

upon which you have focused. V5 is also activated when viewing visual illusions (such as the one in Figure 6.12) that result in the perception of apparent motion. Studies using monkeys with surgical damage confined to V5 have found that these monkeys are unable to discern visual motion. Although exceptionally rare, human cases have been identified where damage resulting from stroke has left patients effectively blind to motion This condition is called **akinetopsia**.

In addition to the visual pathways discussed thus far, there are also pathways emerging from the retina which directly innervate several subcortical structures. One of these pathways innervates a small set of nuclei just above the optic chasm called the suprachiasmatic nucleus (SCN). The SCN is the principle biological pacemaker responsible for coordinating numerous biological rhythms. The 24-hr circadian wake-sleep cycle is one of these biological rhythms. Researchers have learned that under conditions of 24-hr constant dim light or darkness, the normal circadian sleep-wake cycle becomes "free-running"—in other words, the daily circadian cycle becomes approximately 24.5 hours long. Apparently our biological pacemaker is regulated by the daily solar cycle of daylight and darkness. Investigations have recently discovered that a unique set of ganglion cells in the retina possess a photopigment called melanopsin and are themselves responsive to light, particularly wavelengths in the blue region of the spectrum. This may explain another up-until-now puzzling phenomenon associated with blindsight in individuals who are cortically blind as a result of damage to the primary visual cortex. It is common for such individuals to have normal 24 hr circadian rhythms rather than free-running biological pacemakers, unless they are exposed to the same conditions of constant lighting under which the circadian cycle of sighted individuals becomes free-running. Hypothetically, the melanopsin-activated pathway from the retina to the SCN is intact, thereby allowing them to become entrained by light. What are the implications? Well for one thing, this indicates that there are components of the visual system of sighted as well as the visual system of some blind individuals that convey information we are not consciously able to perceive as visual images (See Figure 6.13).

Finally, some closing comments regarding cortical visual perception specifically and sensory perceptual processes in general are required. First of all, the information above only begins to touch upon many of the complexities that have been discovered regarding visual information processing by the brain. From what has been discussed regarding the ventral and dorsal streams, it can also be assumed that information is not shared between the two pathways or that features are processed only sequentially, in one direction. Neither is the case. There is substantial cross-talk between parallel perceptual modules at multiple levels within the visual system as well as within other sensory perceptual systems. There is also a great deal of cross-talk between sensory systems, a phenomenon that enables our auditory perception to influence our visual perceptions and visa versa.

This is particularly evident among individuals who are synesthetes. **Synesthesia** is literally a blending of sensory–perceptual modalities. Individuals with

Akinetopsia

As a child, you may have played with a "flip-book"—a small booklet containing still images that appear to move when you rapidly flip through the pages. Traditional motion pictures and animated cartoons are based upon a comparable assemblage of sequential still images that are rapidly projected onto a screen. If the images are presented quickly enough and with relatively small changes in the position of the actors or the surrounding features, the result is a perception of fluid motion. The brain is able to ignore or infer, depending upon what theory you believe is correct, the gap between the images or the movements that must have occurred during the interval separating the changing scenes.

In a related example of this phenomenon, if you were placed in a totally darkened room and two small lights at one end of the room were briefly lit and extinguished in rapid succession, you would likely have the perception that a single light had moved across the room rather than perceiving the presence of two separate lights. Our visual system has evolved in a manner that allows us to construct or extract information about movement from features in a visual scene and there are specific regions of the visual cortex that are specialized for doing so (e.g., V5).

Just as there are regions of the accessory visual cortex where color and facial features are processed, so are there regions that play critical roles in perception of motion. There have been case reports dating back many centuries of individuals

Fig 6.12 Apparent Motion Perception

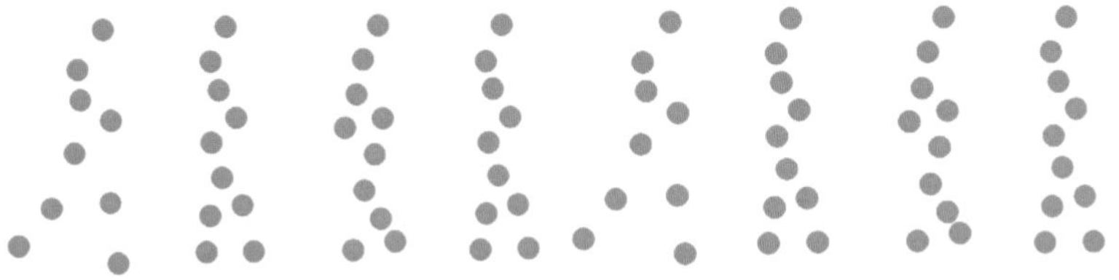

© Infobase Learning

This sequence of static figures is typically interpreted as representing movement of a walking figure. The V5 component of the visual cortex plays an important role in processing stimuli that contribute to such motion perception.

synesthesia may report that they experience sounds accompanied by lights, geometric images, tactile sensations, or even tastes. Arguably, we may each be synesthetes to some extent. Sometimes, a sensory or perceptual deficit in one mode may unmask a synesthetic experience. There is evidence that there is a great deal

who after stroke or other brain injury were left with varying degrees of impairment in perception of movement. However, one of the first case studies to be assessed in great detail and for whom investigators were able to localize cortical damage and map brain activity was that of L.M.—a 43 year-old woman who had suffered an apparent stroke that left her with motion blindness (akinestopia). As noted in her initial case reports, L.M.:

". . . has difficulty, for example, in pouring tea or coffee into a cup because the fluid appeared to be frozen, like a glacier. In addition, she could not stop pouring at the right time since she was unable to perceive the movement in the cup (or pot) when fluid rose.

The report continues . . . In a room where more than two other people were walking she felt very insecure and unwell, and usually left the room immediately, because "people were suddenly here or there but I have not seen them moving."

So to L.M., movements appeared to occur as though they were widely spaced images in a flip-book—with large gaps in the sequence of movements that must have occurred during the interceding period of time. If you have ever watched dancers moving while illuminated only by a strobe light, you may have some impression of the visual world L.M. experienced all the time.

The scans of L.M.'s brain indicated that the region of bilateral damage corresponded with a region identified as V5 in the brain of monkeys. Bilateral surgical damage of V5 results in selective impairments in motion perception similar to those described by L.M. Based upon other cases, there is also evidence that a cortical region adjacent to V5 in the medial temporal lobes (MT+) is activated by visual features that are the hallmarks of movements made by the human body. In these experiments volunteers are dressed in black body suits with LED lights strategically located at key body joints. When viewed in total darkness, the pattern of lights appears random until the volunteers move, at which time they are instantly perceived to be human actors, and activity in MT+ increases.

Akinetopsia is exceptionally rare. But the condition can be transiently replicated in healthy volunteers by using repetitive transcranial magnetic stimulation (rTMS). In rTMS, rapid and repeated brief application of a strong magnetic field above a region of the cortex can temporarily interfere with brain activity in the underlying cortex. When TMS is stopped, normal cortical functions are reinstated. Several studies have shown that TMS directed over V5 induces temporary deficits in motion perception similar to those experienced by L.M.

of cross-modal plasticity between sensory-perceptual systems. For example, there is evidence that the visual cortex of individuals who become blind at an early age recruit regions of the visual cortex to process auditory information. Perhaps this is one reason that blind individuals like Daniel Kish, who was introduced in our

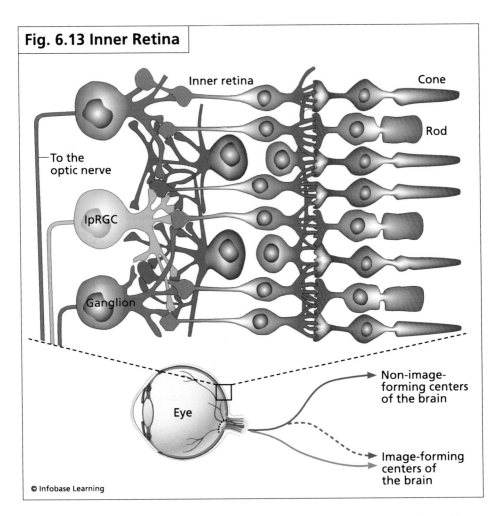

Fig. 6.13 Inner Retina

Inner retina

Cone

Rod

To the optic nerve

IpRGC

Ganglion

Eye

Non-image-forming centers of the brain

Image-forming centers of the brain

© Infobase Learning

A schematic representation of the photoreceptor layer, bipolar cell layer, and ganglion cell layer of the retina. Subgroups of ganglion cells (the ipRGC shaded blue) contain the photopigment melanopsin, thereby making the ganglion cells themselves reactive to light in the blue range of the spectrum. Because this is the predominant wavelength comprising daylight, it may be that this pathway also comprises one of several non-image forming visual systems. Another subcortical non-image forming pathway connects the retina with the midbrain superior colliculus. This system has a role in coordinating our reflexive eye movements in response to movement and sound in the environment.

discussion of the auditory system, are capable of using echolocation to navigate while riding a bike. If it is the case that nervous system plasticity enables auditory sensations to be processed in the visual system and visa versa, then it should be no surprise that some individuals may experience cross-modal synesthesia.

Further Reading

Akiyoshi Kitaoka's Visual Illusions. Available at http://www.ritsumei.ac.jp/~akitaoka/index-e.html. Retrieved November 2011.

Beckers G, and V. Homberg. "Cerebral Visual Motion Blindness: Transitory Akinetopsia Induced by Transcranial Magnetic Stimulation of Human Area V5." *Proceedings of the Royal Society: Biological Sciences* 249, no. 1325 (1992): 173–178.

Corcoran A.J., J.R. Barber, and W.E. Conner . W.E. "Tiger Moth Jams Bat Sonar." *Science* 325 (2009): 325–327.

Czeisler, C.A., T.L. Shanahan, E.B. Klerman, H. Martens, D.J. Bortman, J.S Emens, T. Klein, and J.F. Rizzo. "Suppression of Melatonin Secretion in Some Blind Patients by Exposure to Bright Light." *New England Journal of Medicine* 332 (1995): 6–11.

Formisano, E., D.-S. Kim, F. Di Salle, P.-F. van de Moortele, K. Ugurbil, and R. Goebel. "Mirror-symmetric Tonotopic Maps in Human Primary Auditory Cortex." Neuron 40 (2003): 859–869.

Garstang, M. "Long Distance, Low-frequency Elephant Communication." *Journal of Comparative Physiology: Neuroethology, Sensory, Neural and Behavioral Physiology* 190, no. 10 (2004): 791–805.

Klerman, E.B., T.L. Shanahan, D.J. Brotman, D.W. Rimmer, J.S. Emens, J.F. Rizzo, and C.A. Czeisler. "Photic Resetting of the Human Circadian Pacemaker in the Absence of Conscious Vision." *J. Biol. Rhythms* 17 (2002): 548–555.

Lamb, T.D. "Evolution of the Eye." *Scientific American* 305 (June 2011): 64–69.

Martinez-Conde, S., and S.L. Macknik. "Magic and the Brain." *Scientific American* 299 (Dec 2008): 72–79.

NPR: Close-up on Chuck Close. Available at http://www.npr.org/blogs/picture-show/2010/04/14/125966367/close. Retrieved November 2011.

Provencio, I. "The Hidden Organ in Our Eyes." *Scientific American*, 304 (Apr 2011): 54–59.

Rosenblum, L.D. *See What I'm Saying. The Extraordinary Powers of Our Five Senses.* New York, N.Y.: W.W. Norton, 2010.

Sacks, O. *An Anthropologist on Mars: Seven Paradoxical Tales.* New York, N.Y.: Knopf, 1995.

———. *The Island of the Colorblind.* New York: N.Y.: Knopf, 1997.

Saenz, Lewis, L.B., A.G. Huth, I. Fine, and C. Koch. "Visual Motion Area MT+/V5 Responds to Auditory Motion in Human Sight-recovered Subjects." *Journal of Neuroscience* 28, no. 20 (2008): 5141–5148.

Stephen Colbert Interviews Chuck Close. Available at http://www.colbertnation.com/the-colbert-report-videos/343737/august-12-2010/chuck-close?xrs=share_copy. Retrieved November 2011.

Thomas, C., T.C. Avidan, G. Humphreys, K. Jung, F. Gao, and M. Behrman. "Reduced Structural Connectivity in Ventral Visual Cortex in Congenital Prosopagnosia." *Nature Neuroscience* 12 (2009): 29–31.

V. Ramachandran. The perception of motion. Available at http://www.youtube.com/watch?v=FAAyB5jGx_4&feature=player_embedded. Retrieved November 2011.

Zaidi, F.H., J.T. Hull, S.N. Pierson, K. Wulff, D. Aeschbach, J.J. Gooley, G.C. Brainard, K. Gregory-Evans, J.F. Rizzo, C.A. Czeisler, et al. "Short-wavelength Light Sensitivity of Circadian, Pupillary and Visual Awareness in Blind Humans Lacking a Functional Outer Retina." *Current Biology* 17 (2007): 2122–2128.

Zeki, S. "Cerebral Akinetopsia (Visual Motion Blindness). *Brain* 114 (1991): 811–824.

Zihl, J. d. vonCramon, and N. Mai. "Selective Disturbance of Movement Vision After Bilateral Brain Damage." Brain 106 (1983): 313–340.

CHAPTER 7

PSYCHOACTIVE DRUGS

In Chapter 2 of this volume we reviewed the process of axonal transmission, which is dependent upon the mechanisms that contribute to the resting and action potentials of a neuron. The action potential ultimately results in the release of chemical messengers called neurotransmitters into the synapse between neurons. Therefore although axonal transmission is a bioelectrical process, communication between neurons is largely a biochemical process. Although axonal transmission can be considered to be "all-or-none," synaptic transmission is much more complex and involves numerous synaptic mechanisms that ultimately determine how the presynaptic neuron influences the postsynaptic neuron. In this chapter we will explore these synaptic mechanisms and consider how psychoactive drugs influence synaptic transmission, thought, emotion, and behavior.

Many endogenous chemical messengers influence synaptic transmission. In this chapter we have an opportunity to discuss only a limited number that are considered to be the major neurotransmitters. The majority of psychoactive drugs influence neural activity via effects on the action of these neurotransmitters within synapses. The major neurotransmitters are categorized as either cholinergic, the monoamines (both the catacholamines and the indolamines), amino acids, or neuropeptide neurotransmitters. Table 7.1 lists the principal neurotransmitters in each of these categories. Although these are the major neurotransmitters, note that more than fifty chemical messengers have been found to act as agents involved in regulating synaptic transmission.

TABLE 7.1: **The Major Neurotransmitters**

Category	Neurotransmitter
Cholinergic NT	Acetylcholine
Monoamine NT	
Catecholamines	Norepinephrine
	Dopamine
Indolamines	Serotonin
Amino Acids NT	γ-Amino Butyric Acid (GABA)
Neuropeptide NT	Endorphin
	LEU- Enkephalin
	Dynorphin

The neurotransmitters that are synthesized by neurons are stored in synaptic vesicles in the axon terminal. Synaptic transmission begins when the action potential reaches the axon terminal, causing these synaptic vesicles to migrate toward the cellular membrane of presynaptic neurons. As the vesicles reach the presynaptic membrane they fuse with it; as a result, the neurotransmitter contained in the vesicle is released into the synapse. Next, the neurotransmitter diffuses within the synapse, ultimately reaching the membrane of the postsynaptic neuron. There the neurotransmitter interacts with receptor sites that determine through numerous mechanisms whether the postsynaptic neuron is more or less likely to generate its own action potential. In some instances the postsynaptic neuron may be depolarized, reach its threshold of excitation, and generate an action potential along its axon. In this instance the effect the neurotransmitter has on the postsynaptic membrane is called an **excitatory postsynaptic potential (EPSP)**. Alternatively, a neurotransmitter may influence receptors that cause the postsynaptic neuron to be hyperpolarized, thereby decreasing the chances that the postsynaptic neuron will generate an axon potential. This is an instance in which an **inhibitory postsynaptic potential (IPSP)** occurs at the postsynaptic membrane.

This is the essence of synaptic transmission: A receptor-mediated biochemical communication across the synapse alters the likelihood that activity with a neural circuit is increased or decreased. However there are a multitude of presynaptic and postsynaptic mechanisms that we have yet to examine and are targets for psychoactive drugs. Before considering how psychoactive drugs alter synaptic communication, there are a few common misconceptions regarding synaptic communication via neurotransmission that must be cleared up.

- First, although many textbooks may identify a neurotransmitter as either excitatory or an inhibitory, most neurotransmitters can either increase or decrease neuronal activity depending upon the specific type of receptor in the synapse. For example, there are at least five distinct types of dopamine receptors. Some of these, when activated by dopamine, will result in an increase in neural activity; others will respond to dopamine by decreasing neural activity. Although two neural circuits may both utilize dopamine, different dopamine receptors in these circuits may confer very different functional properties to each circuit.
- A second common misconception is that increased activity within the brain must always result in an observable increase in some action, emotion, or thought. Similarly, decreased activity within the brain is assumed to result in an overt decrease in action, emotion, or thought. This is not the case. Whether neural activity is increased or decreased as a result of a neurotransmitter's influence across a synapse does not necessarily lead to a corresponding influence on behavior displayed by the organism experiencing the neural activity. Decreased activity in a neural circuit may result in an increase in an overt action; increased activity in a circuit may result in a decrease in overt action.
- It is incorrect to assume that only one type of neurotransmitter is released within a synapse. Because multiple neurotransmitters may be released within a synapse, the activity within a pathway may depend upon the overall influence of multiple neurotransmitters and multiple receptors. Additionally, many pathways that utilize different neurotransmitters may be interconnected in complex ways. Thus it is an oversimplification to assume that changes in any behavioral, emotional, or cognitive state is attributed to changes in availability or release of a single neurotransmitter.
- The mechanisms that mediate synaptic transmission are not static. They are dynamic—constantly changing as a consequence of their inputs and outputs. Developmental changes occur across the lifespan, both within and between neural systems. Consequently the mechanisms that govern responsiveness to neurotransmitters and drugs may change, from minute-to-minute, day-to-day, etc. For example, the density of receptors and type of receptors may change with time. Such changes may contribute to phenomena such as **drug tolerance** and **drug sensitivity**.

Keeping these points in mind, we will review the synaptic mechanisms involved in chemical communication across synapses. Psychoactive substances and medications work via their effects on these mechanisms.

NEUROTRANSMITTER SYNTHESIS

Each neuron generates the available quantity of neurotransmitter(s) it releases within itself. We do not need to go into the details of this here except to say that the biochemical processes involved in neurotransmitter synthesis require molecules that are precursors and that are converted into each neurotransmitter by enzymes within the neuron. For example, the precursor for both catecholamine neurotransmitters is tyrosine. **Tyrosine** is an amino acid that is contained in various foods that you eat. Tyrosine from your meals enters your circulatory system and is eventually transported into the brain where it is converted into an intermediate precursor of dopamine by the enzyme **tyrosine hydroxylase**. Only neurons that manufacture this enzyme can do this. To make dopamine from the intermediate precursor requires a second enzyme (**aromatic amino acid decarboxylase**), and yet another enzyme (**dopamine-β-hydroxylase**) is required to convert dopamine into norepinephrine. The important point to consider is that diet and the availability of these enzymes can affect the chemical messages that occur between neurons. Dietary substances or drugs that alter the availability of precursors of the neurotransmitter(s) or enzymes required for their synthesis can have profound effects on brain functions.

VESICULAR STORAGE

Once synthesis is complete, neurotransmitters are stored within synaptic vesicles. This ensures that the neurotransmitter is not altered or degraded by other enzymatic processes before it is released into the synapse. Some psychoactive substances and drugs can affect this storage, influencing the transport of a neurotransmitter from the cytoplasm into the vesicle or the ability of the vesicle to keep a neurotransmitter from moving back into the cytoplasm, where is may be enzymatically degraded. An example of this is **reserpine**, which interferes with function of transport mechanisms responsible for transporting the monoamines into vesicles. The result is that the monoamines remaining in the cytoplasm are subject to enzymatic transformation or degradation, ultimately reducing the amount of neurotransmitter that is released into the synapse following the action potential.

NEUROTRANSMITTER RELEASE

Once an action potential reaches the axon terminal, the entry of calcium ions (Ca) that accompany the influx of sodium ions (Na) initiates a cascade of complex processes that cause the vesicles to fuse with the presynaptic membrane and release their contents into the synapse. Any substances that interfere with this can impair or halt synaptic transmission. Conversely, other drugs can alter synaptic transmission by facilitating the processes involved in neurotransmitter release. Amphetamines (powerful psychoactive stimulants) work in this way. They trigger an excessive release of the monoamine neurotransmitters dopamine and norepinephrine, and to lesser extent, the release of serotonin. Subcutaneous injections of Botox®, which is used cosmetically to hide facial wrinkles, work by blocking release of acetylcholine within nerves, thus innervating facial muscles.

POSTSYNAPTIC NEUROTRANSMITTER RECEPTORS

Membrane proteins that function as neurotransmitter receptors mediate the effects of synaptic neurotransmitters on postsynaptic neurons. As noted above, there are different types of receptors for each neurotransmitter and multiple receptor subtypes for a specific neurotransmitter. The type of receptor in the postsynaptic membrane determines whether the neurotransmitter elicits an excitatory or inhibitory postsynaptic potential.

Some psychoactive drugs influence brain functioning by altering the manner by which neurotransmitters affect postsynaptic receptors. They may mimic the effects of the neurotransmitter or they may block the neurotransmitter's effect on the receptor. In some instances drugs that mimic neurotransmitters at these receptors have much more pronounced effects than the neurotransmitter itself.

The first generation antipsycholtic medications (e.g., Thorazine®, Haldol®) included drugs that are very potent dopamine receptor blockers. Interestingly, powerful stimulants such as the amphetamines stimulate synaptic release of dopamine, and some of the symptoms experienced by chronic abusers of amphetamine are similar to some symptoms of schizophrenia (**amphetamine-induced psychosis**). A significant adverse side-effect that is common among patients taking first-generation antipsychotics is **Tardive Dyskinesia**. Tardive dyskinesia is characterized by the emergence of involuntary movements, particularly of the facial muscles; in extreme cases, side-effects include tremors and movements of the arms and legs. The latest generation of antipsychotics medications (e.g., Clozaril® and Respirdol®) block a different dopamine receptor than first-generation drugs do and also block some serotonin receptors. The combined actions are more effective at reducing symptoms of schizophrenia for some patients and are less likely to cause tardive dyskinesia.

PRESYNAPTIC NEUROTRANSMITTER RECEPTORS

Neurotransmitter receptors are also found in the presynaptic membrane. Such receptors are called autoreceptors. Consider why this may be. What function might you expect these receptors to serve? The answer may be as simple as understanding why you have both a mouth and ears. When you engage in conversation, isn't it helpful to hear what you say as well as what is said to you? Suppose you misspeak. Having heard what you said provides you with feedback allowing you to alter your subsequent sentences and correct yourself. The communication that occurs across synapses is a dynamic process—just as dynamic as the conversations you have with others. The function of presynaptic receptors is analogous to the function your ears serve. Each allows for regulating communication, depending on feedback about the message that has previously been sent.

Autoreceptors provide the presynaptic neuron with feedback about the status of neurotransmitter levels in the synapse. If the neurotransmitter level in the synapse is excessive, stimulation of autoreceptors inhibits further release of that neurotransmitter. In this instance, although the presynaptic neuron may generate an action potential, little or no neurotransmitter is released. When the autoreceptors are not activated, neurotransmitter release is uninhibited; each action potential results in additional neurotransmitter release. You can think of autoreceptors as emergency brakes that may be applied to diminish the release of a neurotransmitter when levels of the neurotransmitter within the synapse are excessive.

There are a number of psychoactive substances that either mimic or block the effects of neurotransmitters on autoreceptors. Think carefully of the consequence of taking a drug that activates autoreceptors. The result would be equivalent to instances when there was an excessive release of neurotransmitter. How should this affect further release of a neurotransmitter? Such a drug should diminish or block release. This may be therapeutic if neural activity witnn this neural circuit had been excessive. How might therapists intervene if neural activity was lower than optimal? One approach might be to prescribe a drug capable of *blocking* activation of autoreceptors, thereby reducing limits on the amount of neurotransmitter that is released to obtain a therapeutic response.

Autoreceptors play an important role in regulating the release of neurotransmitters. But the amount of neurotransmitter within a synapse is also regulated by presynaptic reuptake mechanisms.

REUPTAKE

Suppose the presynaptic vesicular supply of neurotransmitter has been depleted. Wouldn't it be efficient if the excess neurotransmitter in the synapse could be recycled, repackaged into vesicles, and made available for release? Reuptake accomplishes this. Reuptake transporters in the presynaptic membrane convey the neurotransmitter in the synapse back into the presynaptic neuron where vesicular transporters replenish the vesicular stores of the neurotransmitter. Some psychoactive substances work either by blocking presynaptic reuptake or in some cases reversing reuptake (See ADHD Sidebar). In either case the neurotransmitter level in the synapse will be elevated or remain high as long as sufficient neurotransmitter is synthesized to sustain the normal levels of release. The antidepressant Prozac® (fluoxetine) is perhaps the most widely recognized reuptake blocker. Some reuptake blockers have similar ability to block all monoamine reuptake transporters, but what is special about Prozac® is that it is a selective serotonin reuptake blocker.

SYNAPTIC ENZYMATIC DEGRADATION/INACTIVATION

Reuptake is one means by which high levels of neurotransmitter in the synapse may be reduced. Another mechanism that has a similar function is enzymatic degradation/inactivation. Although synthetic enzymes play a role in the production of neurotransmitters from precursor molecules, there are also enzymes that can metabolize neurotransmitters into their original precursor molecules. An example is acetylcholinesterase (AChE), an enzyme that metabolizes the neurotransmitter acetylcholine. Different metabolic enzymes metabolize other types of neurotransmitter. The monamine neurotransmitters, for example, are metabolized by **monamine oxidases** A and B (MAOA & MAOB).

Some psychoactive substances work by inhibiting the processes of enzymatic degradation, thereby sustaining high levels of neurotransmitter within the synapse. Examples of these are the medications Cognex® and Aricept®. These are typically prescribed to treat individuals experiencing the early stage cognitive impairments of Alzheimer disease. Both drugs are AchE inhibitors.

SYNAPTIC NEUROTRANSMITTER AGONISTS AND ANTAGONISTS

Psychoactive substances may be categorized in a number of ways. They may be categorized as neurotransmitters are characterized—according to their molecular structure/composition. More commonly they are categorized according to their therapeutic or behavioral and cognitive effects (e.g., as hallucinogens, antidepressants, stimulants, analgesics). Another way to categorize these substances is based on how they affect synaptic transmission.

Agonists are drugs that facilitate the effects a neurotransmitter has on the postsynaptic neuron. Drugs that facilitate neurotransmitter release, inhibit enzymatic degradation, block reuptake, and activate postsynaptic receptors are considered agonists of synaptic transmission. Thus Prozac® is considered a serotonin agonist; Cognex® is an acetylcholine agonist. Notably, agonists also include drugs that block synaptic autoreceptors. Because activation of autoreceptors inhibits release, blocking these receptors enables release to continue unimpeded, ultimately increasing neurotransmitter levels in the synapse and initially facilitating synaptic communication.

Antagonists impede or block the effects a neurotransmitter has on the postsynaptic neuron. Antagonists include drugs that block postsynaptic receptors, inhibit neurotransmitter synthesis, impair vesicular storage, or block release. A drug that activates autoreceptors is also an antagonist because it decreases neurotransmitter release from the presynaptic neuron.

These two terms require a brief cautionary note. As you read other texts and research articles that describe the synaptic mechanisms of various psychoactive substances, it is important to recognize that the meaning of the terms agonist

Attention Deficit Hyperactivity Disorder

Over the previous two decades, there has been a remarkable and troubling increase in the prevalence of Attention Deficit Disorder (ADD) and Attention Deficit Hyperactivity Disorder (ADHD). According to statistics collected by the Centers for Disease Control and Prevention, the number of children with parent-reported diagnosis of ADHD increased by 22 percent from 2003 to 2007. This trend has continued. At present, more and more children are being diagnosed with ADD/ADHD and at a younger age. There is also an increase in the number of adults diagnosed with these conditions. Contemporary estimates indicate that ADHD is diagnosed in 8 percent of children aged 4 to 17 and in 2.9 to 4.4 percent of adults (NIDA NOTES, June 2009).

There is no single explanation for the escalating number of individuals diagnosed with these conditions, but it is likely that numerous factors contribute to the likelihood that someone will be diagnosed as having ADD/ADHD. A 2010 article published in the journal *Pediatrics* summarized the results of a study that implicated early exposure to pesticides as one risk factor. Other studies have identified markers for candidate genes associated with ADHD. Because males are at least twice as likely to be diagnosed with ADHD, gender is certainly a contributing factor.

Along with the increased prevalence of ADHD there has been a corresponding precipitous increase in the sale of prescription medications to treat the condition. Paradoxically, the most frequently prescribed medications for ADHD are the stimulants methylphenidate (Ritalin®, Concerta®) and amphetamine (Adderall®). Both are dopamine agonists that increase synaptic levels of dopamine, however, their mechanisms of action within the synapse differ. Methylphenidate blocks reuptake of dopamine via the dopamine transporter (DAT), elevating the amount of dopamine that remains in the synapse due to vesicular release. Amphetamine actually reverses the DAT mechanism, thereby adding to the dopamine that has already been released into the synapse via vesicles. Several theories have been suggested to explain the paradoxical effects of these stimulants in the treatment of ADHD, but which of these is accurate has yet to be determined. According to one theory, dopamine levels within a specific brain circuit are deficient, and the stimulant medications raise levels of dopamine and facilitate neurotransmission within this circuit. According to another theory, in ADHD, dopaminergic transmission in a different circuit is overactive. By blocking/reversing reuptake of dopamine, the synaptic levels of dopamine and antagonist may vary depending upon the author and the topic. This can be confusing and understanding the terms in different contexts requires attention to detail. In some instances a drug that activates any of the mechanisms we

rise until they reach levels that activate autoreceptors, thereby inhibiting release of dopamine and ultimately resulting in a paradoxical decrease in activity within this previously hyperactive neural circuit.

Given currently available findings, it seems that some type of dysfunctional synaptic regulation of dopamine circuits in the brain is involved. However, other neurotransmitter systems may be involved as well. Atomoxetine (Strattera®), which selectively blocks reuptake of norepinephrine, is an alternative ADHD medication that works best for certain individuals.

Fig. 7.1 Chemical Similarities between Stimulants and Dopamine

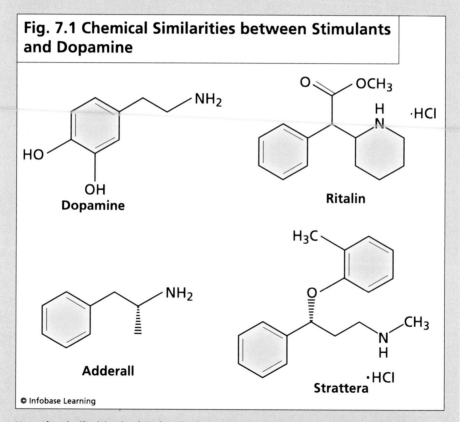

© Infobase Learning

Note the similarities in the chemical structures of dopamine and the dopamine agonists Ritalin (methyphenidate) and Adderall (Amphetimine). The alternative medication Strattera (Atomoxetine) selectively blocks reuptake of norepinephrine and is structurally somewhat different from Ritalin and Adderall.

have reviewed may be identified as an agonist, regardless of the ultimate effect on synaptic transmission. In such instances the topic of focus is the synaptic mechanism, not synaptic transmission. The same caveat applies to the use of the term antagonist. The context will dictate whether the term applies to the effect the drug has on a synaptic mechanism or on synaptic transmission.

ACUTE VERSUS CHRONIC EFFECTS OF PSYCHOACTIVE SUBSTANCES

It is important to recognize that each of the mechanisms of synaptic transmission are dynamic, that they are subject to change. The number and type of postsynaptic receptors can vary. So can the number and type of receptors that are found in the presynaptic and postsynaptic membranes, which may increase or decrease. This is referred to as receptor up-regulation and down-regulation, respectively. Let us consider what this may mean.

First, let's suppose someone is given a prescription for one of the first generation antipsychotic medications that block a specific type of dopamine receptor. The very first time the person takes this medication, acute effects on synaptic mechanisms may occur within several hours. The medication effectively blocks some receptors and alters synaptic transmission. Nonetheless, it may take several days or weeks for the drug to block the number of receptors that must be blocked to produce tangible therapeutic outcomes. This desirable outcome may persist for weeks, months, and even years with occasional adjustments in the dose of the drug. Adjustments in the dosage may be necessary because long-term treatment is likely to create dynamic changes in synaptic mechanisms.

Long-term treatment with the dopamine receptor blocker may, for example, result in an up-regulation in the number of the targeted receptors. This might require increasing the dose of the drug to maintain its therapeutic efficacy. This sequence describes the phenomenon of tolerance, which in essence is the body's ability to adjust to a substance over time until the initial effect the substance had on the body diminishes or even disappears. In some instances the increased dosage required to reestablish the desired effect becomes so great that it produces undesirable side-effects that the patient cannot tolerate or that seriously compromise the patient's general health. When this happens, it may be possible to prescribe another medication that has a similar effect on synaptic transmission but accomplishes this by influencing a different synaptic mechanism. For example, our hypothetical patient may benefit from transition to an alternative antipsychotic medication, perhaps one of the latest generation of medications that block a different subset of dopamine receptors as well as some serotonin receptors. Not all patients develop drug tolerance. On the contrary, some patients develop an increased sensitivity to a medication, and this may require decreasing the dose of medication prescribed. Here again it is important to remember that synaptic functions and their related processes are dynamic, and this can be the reason for both tolerance and heightened sensitivity.

Now that you have an appreciation for the dynamic nature of synaptic responses to acute and long-term use of medications, see if you can explain why the therapeutic influence of many antidepressants typically occurs only after two or three weeks of treatment. To focus the exercise, let's consider a specific type of drug, the widely prescribed antidepressant Prozac®. Prozac®. effectively blocks a significant number of serotonin reuptake transporters within hours after a patient has taken the first pill. Almost immediately the acute effects of the medication increase the levels of serotonin in serotonergic neural pathways. So why do most patients experience relief from their depression only after taking their medication for another few weeks? Think of some explanations before reading further.

Hopefully you have concluded that there are several dynamic changes in synaptic mechanism that can plausibly account for the delayed efficacy of the medication. Investigators have explored a number of these, but one explanation that is supported by the majority of studies is that the therapeutic effects of an antidepressant serotonin agonist such as Prozac® are most correlated with a quantifiable down-regulation in serotonin autoreceptors. One theory based on this explanation attributes the effectiveness of serotonergic antidepressants to the diminished negative feedback influence of autoreceptors on synaptic release of serotonin. According to this theory the increase levels of serotonin that result from blocking its reuptake eventually desensitize serotonin autoreceptors, thereby raising the levels of serotonin in the synapse that previously had been required to inhibit continued release.

Thus far we have encountered several examples of psychotherapeutic medication and examined their influences on mechanisms of synaptic transmission. Table 7.2 summarized these and several others. Note that some antidepressants are also effective at treating general anxiety disorder. This is just a small sample of medications that have been approved by the Food and Drug Administration (FDA) for treatment of these and other psychological conditions.

RECREATIONAL DRUGS. MISUSE OF DRUGS, AND DRUG ABUSE

We can alter synaptic transmission simply through day-to-day and minute-to-minute interactions with stimuli in our environments. For example, the people we interact with, the behaviors we engage in, the foods we consume, and just about anything we would typically encounter in our environments can in some way alter synaptic transmission. For example, things that we find rewarding and pleasurable generally increase activity in several neural pathways within the brain that chiefly employ the neurotransmitter dopamine. This neural mechanism is adaptive in that the things we generally perceive to be rewarding or pleasurable, such as friendly social interactions that may

TABLE 7.2
Common Psychotherapeutic Medications

Disorder	Medications	Mechanism of Action	Agonist/ Antagonist
Depression	Celexa, Paxil, Prozac, Zoloft	SSRI	Agonist
	Cymbalta, Effexor, Elavil	SNRI	Agonist
	Marplan, Nardil.	MAOi	Agonist
Schizophrenia	Haldol, Thorazine	DR Blocker	Antagonist
	Clozaril, Respiridal	DR/SERTR Blocker	Antagonist
ADHD	Adderall, Ritalin, Straterra	DA or NE Release	Agonist
General Anxiety Disorder	Librium, Valium, Xanax	GABAR Mimic/ Activator	Agonist
	Celexa, Marplan, Paxil, Prozac	SSRI	Agonist
Alzheimer Disease	Aricept, Cognex	AchE Inhibitor	Agonist

AchE = Acetylcholinesterase
DR = Dopamine Receptor
GABAR = GABA Receptor
MAOi = Monamineoxidase Inhibitor
SERTR = Serotonin Receptor
SSRI – Selective Serotonin Reuptake Inhibitor
SNRI = Serotonin/Norepinephrine Reuptake Inhibitor

facilitate pro-social or altruistic behaviors, can contribute to our general well being and health.

However, excessive actuation of this same reward system is not necessarily a good thing. Consider addiction, for example. Although it is possible that the risk of addiction is nothing new, people living in today's societies face numerous environmental stimuli that are many times more capable of activating our neural reward pathways than those stimuli encountered by our ancestors. Granted, there are natural substances that possess psychoactive and addictive properties (e.g., ethanol from natural fermentation), but people have also found ways to refine or synthesize substances with far greater reward potency than those substances our ancestors might have encountered. Cocaine, Oxycodone, heroine, and methamphetamine are just a few examples of today's psychoactive substances. Although some of these drugs have therapeutic properties when properly used (i.e., under the supervision of a qualified health professional), they also pose substantial risk of addiction when misused.

One reward pathway that has been implicated in addictive disorders originates from a region within our midbrain called the ventral tegmental area (VTA) and terminates in the nucleus accumbens (nACC) in the forebrain. As mentioned above, the neurons in this pathway communicate with each other at synapses where the principle neurotransmitter is dopamine. Research has found that the addictive properties of a drug are generally correlated with the degree to which the drug stimulates the release of dopamine at synapses in this pathway. The more rapidly the drug stimulates release of dopamine (and the greater the level of this release), the greater the risk of abuse and addiction.

You may wonder about other forms of addiction, particularly patterns of behavior that some investigators consider behavioral addictions that have received recent attention, such as excessive and compulsive Internet use, gambling, and computer gaming. If you apply the reward-based concept of synaptic transmission, this is indeed a logical supposition. For example, some studies have shown that video games can activate the same reward pathways as those that are stimulated by addictive drugs. There is also some evidence that lower than normal activation in these circuits may make someone more vulnerable to behavioral addictions because the activation they achieve via their compulsions is so much more rewarding. Lastly, some medications that have been proven useful in treating substance abuse disorders have also been found to help individuals with apparent behavioral addictions.

Further Reading

Edmund S., and E.S. Higgins. "Do ADHD Drugs Take a Toll on the Brain?" *Scientific American Mind* 20 (Jul 2009): 38–43.

Ettinger, R.H. *Psychopharmacology.* New York, NY: Prentice Hall, 2010.

Holden C. " 'Behavioral' Addictions: Do the Exist?" *Science,* 294, no. 5544 (2001): 980-982.

Julien, R.M., C.D. Advokat, and J. Comaty. *A Primer of Drug Action.* 12th ed. New York, NY: Worth Publishers, 2001.

M. J. Koepp, R. N. Gunn, A. D. Lawrence, V. J. Cunningham, A. Dagher, T. Jones, D. J. Brooks, C. J. Bench & P. M. Grasby. "Evidence for Striatal Dopamine release During a Video Game." *Nature,* 393, no. 6682 (1998): 266-

Nemeroff, C.B. "The Neurobiology of Depression." *Scientific American* 278 (Jun 1998): 42–49.

Reuter, J., Raedler, T., Rose, M., Hand, I., Gläscher, J., and Büchel, C. "Pathological Gambling is Linked to Reduced Activation of the Mesolimbic Reward System." *Nature Neuroscience*, 8, no 2 (2005): 147-148.

The National Institute of Drug Abuse (NIDA). Available at http://www.nida.nih.gov/nidahome.html. Retrieved November 2011.

The National Institute of Mental Health (NIMH) : Mental health Medications. Available at http://www.nimh.nih.gov/health/publications/mental-health-medications/complete-index.shtml - pub11

The New Science of Addiction: Genetics and the Brain. Available at http://learn.genetics.utah.edu/content/addiction/. Retrieved November 2011.

Wenner, M. "A New Kind of Target." *Scientific American* 301 (Aug 2009): 70–76.

Westly, E. "Different Shades of Blue." *Scientific American Mind* 21 (May 2010): 30–37.

GLOSSARY

acetylcholine (ACh)   One of the primary neurotransmitter molecules, ACh is the neurotransmitter that stimulates muscle contraction of striated voluntary skeletal muscles.

ageusia   Loss or one or more of the sensory qualities of taste (umami, sweet, salty, bitter, and sour).

akinetopsia   A condition in which cortical damage results in an inability to perceive motion.

amino acid neurotransmitters   Evolutionarily likely to be among the first neurotransmitter molecules; these include gamma amino butyric acid (GABA), glutamate, glycine, and aspartate.

amphetamine-induced psychosis   Repeated abuse of stimulants that are potent facilitators of dopamine synaptic transmission; can result in symptoms, such as schizophrenia, that may be difficult to distinguish from a psychoses (e.g., paranoia, delusions, and hallucinations).

Amyotrophic Lateral Sclerosis (ALS)   A neurodegenerative disorder that results in the death of motor neurons within the spinal cord and cerebral cortex, inevitably culminating in the loss of control over voluntary actions and ultimately death. It is also known in the United States as Lou Gehrig's disease, after the famous member of the New York Yankees who was diagnosed with the disease. Theoretical physicists Steven Hawking is among the longest surviving individuals with ALS.

anosmia   A decrease or total absence of olfactory sensory acuity.

aromatic amino acid decarboxylase   A critical enzyme in the synthetic pathway from tyrosine to dopamine.

autoreceptors   Neurotransmitter receptors that are located on the presynaptic neuron and mediate the release of neurotransmitter from the presynaptic neuron via negative feedback, thus inhibiting further release of neurotransmitter.

autosomal chromosomes   In humans these constitute 22 of the 23 pairs of chromosomes, all except for the pair of sex chromosomes.

binding problem   The absences of a clear understanding of how the brain integrates multiple modes of sensory and cognitive information.

blindsight   A rare condition that occurs in some individuals who have been blinded as a result of stroke or damage to the primary visual cortices and still retain the ability to respond to visual cues of movement and in some instances the location of objects.

Capgras Syndrome   Also known as Capgras Illusion; a condition in which the afflicted individual possesses the belief that another individual or close family member has been replaced by an imposter who is a nearly perfect replicate of the individual replaced.

cones   Cone shaped sensory neurons within the retina that are selectively responsive to the wavelength of light (color). There are three types of cones, each of which is maximally responsive to a different wavelength of light (nanometers; nm)—blue (420 nm), green (533 nm), and red (560 nm)—and contribute primarily to our visual perception under high illumination conditions, e.g., in daylight.

dermatomes   Tactile receptive fields of individual receptors that collectively contribute to the fibers that form a single spinal sensory nerve; each dermatome corresponds to a specific strip (band) of skin.

Diffusor Tensor Imaging (DTI)   One of several non-invasive neural imaging technologies that are specialized for visualizing internal anatomical features of the central nervous system. In this case, DTI is useful for visualizing so-called white matter, which is composed of myelinated neuronal pathways.

dopamine-β-hydroxylase   An enzyme required for the final step in the synthetic pathway from tyrosine to norepinephrine.

drug tolerance and sensitivity   Tolerance is a decrease in responsiveness to a drug following repeated exposure/use, whereas sensitivity is an enhanced response to the drug following repeated exposure/use.

electroencephalography (EEG)   A means of visualizing the changing patterns of neural activity from a multitude of cortical neurons via electrodes that are placed on the surface of the head.

epigenome   Literally, the components of the genome that surround genes. Modifications of the epigenome by the environment, diet, and experience can modify the pattern of expression of genes throughout the lifespan.

Excitatory Post-Synaptic Potential (EPSP)   An EPSP occurs when a neurotransmitter activates a receptor on the post-synaptic neuron resulting in depolarization of the resting potential of the post-synaptic neuron.

family-based linkage analysis   A strategy for assessing the genetic contributions to diseases by examining the multigenerational patterns of gene inheritance and expression in families with multiple afflicted individuals.

fusiform face area (FFA)   A region in the inferior temporal lobes of the brain containing cells that are responsive to complex images corresponding to faces (see prosopagnosia).

ghrelin   A hormone produced by the stomach; has been shown to contribute to the feeling of hunger. Ghrelin levels increase before meals and decrease after meals.

Huntington disease (HD)   Also know as Huntington's Chorea (dance); devastating neurodegenerative disorder in humans that is caused by altered functioning of genes located on chromosome 4. An autosomal dominant disorder, HD belongs to a group of trinucleotide repeat disorders, in which a sequence of three DNA nucleotides are repeated an unusually high number of times. Normally, a portion of chromosome 4 contains a CAG trinucleotide sequence that repeats 10 to 28 times. But in persons with Huntington disease, the sequence is repeated 36 to 120 times, disrupting normal gene expression.

hyperosmia   An increased is sensory acuity for odors, in some cases hyperosmia occurs in response to specific compounds (e.g., isovaleric acid).

hypogeusia   Exceptionally high and atypical gustatory (taste) sensitivity/acuity.

Inhibitory Post-Synaptic Potential (IPSP)   An IPSP occurs when a neurotransmitter activates a receptor on the post-synaptic neuron resulting in hyperpolarization of the resting potential of the post-synaptic neuron.

interoception   Perception of the internal sensory state of one's own body.

kinesthesia   Perception of the relative motion of parts of one's own body in relation to each other.

lateral geniculate nucleus (LGN)   A nucleus within the thalamus of the brain containing input from both the left and right eyes within the primary visual pathway leading to the primary visual cortex in the occipital lobe. (see parvocellular and magnocellular LGN) leptin (LPTN) A hormone produced by adipose (fat) cells and involved in the regulation of feeding and weight. Deficits in leptin or leptin insensitivity have been shown to be associated with obesity.

magnetoencephalography (MEG) A non-invasive neural imaging technique that measures the weak magnetic fields generated by neuronal activity of the brain.

magnocellular LGN Two distinct cellular layers of the lateral geniculate nucleus (LGN), each containing cells with relatively large soma and dendritic fields. The magnocellular cells in these layers receive inputs from rods cells in either the left or right eye.

mitral cells Sensory neurons that convey olfactory information from glomeruli within the olfactory bulbs to the primary olfactory cortex (pyriform cortex).

monoamine neurotransmitters Neurotransmitters that contain a single amine ring structure; these include the catecholamines (dopamine and norepinephrine) and the indolamine (serotonin).

monoamine oxidases Enzymes that degrade/metabolize monoamine neurotransmitters.

myelin The lipid insulation enveloping some neuronal axons and facilitating the speed at which action potentials are transmitted along the axon (see oligodendroglia and Schwann cells).

neuropeptide neurotransmitter Neurotransmitters that consist of long sequences of amino acid. These sequences are not as long as those that comprise proteins. The endogenous opioids (endorphins, enkephalins, dynorphins) are examples of neuropeptide neurotransmitters.

nociceptors Primary pain receptors.

olfactory glomeruli Each olfactory glomeruli in the olfactory bulbs receives information from many sensory nerves within the olfactory mucosa lining the nasal cavity.

oligodendroglia Cells that form the myelin sheath covering axons in the central nervous system.

opponent-process hypothesis An alternative to the trichromatic theory of color perception. According to this theory, color vision results from the pattern of activation of retinal cells in a spectrally opponent manner—i.e., having opposite responses to light of different wavelengths.

optic radiations The tracts within the visual system that convey information from the lateral geniculate nucleus (LGN) to the primary visual cortex in each cerebral hemisphere.

Organ of Corti (OC)   The component structure of the cochlea of the inner ear; contains the sensory receptors that respond to vibrations of a specific frequency/pitch.

parvocellular LGN   The four distinct cellular layers of the lateral geniculate nucleus (LGN) containing cells with relatively small soma and dendritic fields. The parvocellular cells within these layers receive inputs from cones in either the left or right eye.

phantom limb phenomenon   The perception that an amputated limb is still intact and may be capable of movement and tactile perception, including perception of painful stimuli. A phenomenon that may be at least somewhat attributable to cortical plasticity following loss of the limb.

phenylthiocarbamide (PTC)   A bitter tasting compound that, like Propylthiouracil (PROP), is commonly employed to identify individuals who have an extremely sensitive sense of taste (i.e., supertasters), particularly for compounds perceived as bitter.

pheromone   A chemical signal that is produced by one individual and excreted into the environment where it effects either the behavior or phsiology of another individual of the same species.

photopic vision   Vision under conditions of high illumination (color), which is mediated primarily by retinal cones cells.

Positron Emission Tomography (PET)   One of several non-invasive neural imaging technologies that are specialized for visualizing patterns of neural activity throughout the brain. In this case, PET is useful for visualizing localized patterns of neuronal activity, based upon the accumulation of specific radioactive tracer molecules in the most active areas of the brain.

Prader-Willi Syndrome (PWS)   A genetic disorder affecting children; associated with genes located on chromosome 15 and results in many symptoms, including extreme feelings of hunger that can manifest in severe obesity. Some PWS children engage in pica, the consumption of non-nutritive substances (e.g., clay, pebbles, sand).

primary visual cortex   The portion of the occipital cortex containing cells responsive to simple visual features, such as differently illuminated lines or borders between regions within the visual field.

proprioception   Perception of the relative position of one's own body in relation to others and the surrounding environment.

propylthiouracil (PROP)   A bitter tasting compound which "supertasters" are acutely responsive to and find extremely unpleasant (see PTC).

prosopagnosia   Also known as face-blindness, a condition in which individuals with otherwise normal visual acuity experience great difficulty in identifying individuals based upon facial appearance. It is most often associated with damage within the fusiform face area (FFA).

receptive fields   The receptive field of a sensory neuron is the area in which stimulation leads to response of a particular sensory neuron, e.g., each rod and cone in the retina is most responsive to light within a specific region in the visual field, that is, within its receptive field.

reserpine   A monoamine neurotransmitter antagonists that works by impairing storage of dopamine, norepinephrine and serotonin within synaptic vesicles in preparation for their release; thereby decreasing the amount of these monoamines that are available for release within neuronal synapses.

retina   The layers of cells at the back of each eye that contribute to the earliest stages of visual perception: photoreceptors, bipolar cells, ganglion cells, amacrine cells, and horizontal cells.

rods   Rod shaped sensory neurons within the retina that are relatively insensitive to the wavelength of light (color) and contribute primarily to visual perception under low illumination conditions, e.g., at night.

Schwann cells   These cells form the myelin sheath covering axons in the peripheral nervous system.

scotopic vision   Vision under conditions of low illumination (black and white), which is mediated primarily by retinal rod cells.

sex chromosomes   In mammals, the X and Y chromosomes. Homozygous (XX) individuals are genetic females, whereas heterozygous (XY) are genetic males.

Single Photon Emission Computed Tomography (SPECT)   One of several non-invasive neural imaging technologies specialized for visualizing patterns of neural activity throughout the brain. SPECT, like PET, measures the accumulation of specific radioactive tracer molecules in the most active areas of the brain.

synesthesia   Multimodal sensory perception involving the blending or combination of inputs from discrete sensory modalities; e.g., hearing colors, tasting shapes, smelling tones.

Tardive Dyskinesia   A syndrome characterized by repetitive, purposeless movements, often of the lips and mouth, that generally results from prolonged use of neuroleptic drugs; in some cases the syndrome can appear after short-term use.

tetrodotoxin (TTX)   A selective voltage-gated sodium channel blocker found in several species of fish (e.g., puffer fish, triggerfish). By blocking the sodium channel, TTX blocks the influx of sodium into the neuron that occurs during the initiation of the neuronal action potential.

Transcranial Magnetic Stimulation (TMS)   TMS involves the non-invasive targeted application of powerful magnetic fields that alter patterns of neural activity. Although used therapeutically, TMS technology has also been utilized as a research tool to examine the function of the brain.

trichromatic hypotheses   A theory of color vision first proposed by Hermann von Helmholtz; posits that human color perception results from the combined inputs from each of the three different types of retinal cone cells. (see Opponent-process hypothesis).

tyrosine   An amino acid that is a precursor for the catecholamine neurotransmitters dopamine and norepinephrine.

umami   One of five primary sensory qualities that contribute to taste perception, umami is associated with rich/savory quality of tastes.

visual photo pigments   The light responsive pigments involved in the earliest stages of sensory transduction of light into neural impulses within the visual system. The photo pigment found in rod cells is rhodopsin. There are three types of cones, each containing an opsin that is maximally responsive to a different wavelength of light.

visual photoreceptors   Cells in the retina capable of transducing light into neural impulses. These include the rods responsible for scotopic (low illumination/black and white) vision and the cones responsible for photopic (high illumination/color) vision. Recent evidence suggests that some bipolar cells also function as photoreceptors.

BIBLIOGRAPHY

Bartoshuk L.M, V.B. Duffy, and I.J. Miller. "PTC/PROP Tasting: Anatomy, Psychophysics, and Sex Effects." *Physiology and Behavior* 56 (1994): 1165– 1171.

Bean, B.P. "The Action Potential in Mammalian Central Neurons." *Nature Reviews Neuroscience* 8 (2007): 451–465.

Beckers G, and V. Homberg. "Cerebral Visual Motion Blindness: Transitory Akinetopsia Induced by Transcranial Magnetic Stimulation of Human Area V5." *Proceedings of the Royal Society: Biological Sciences* 249, no. 1325 (1992): 173–178.

Blakemore, S.J., D.M. Wolpert, and C.D. Firth. "Central Cancellation of Self-produced Tickle Sensation." *Nature Neuroscience* 1 (1998): 635–640.

Carlson, N.R. *Physiology of Behavior*. 10th ed. New York, N.Y.: Allyn & Bacon, 2010.

Carter, R. *The Human Brain Book*. New York, N.Y.: DK Publishing, 2009.

Carter, C.S., and L.L. Getz. "Monogomy and the Prairie Vole." *Scientific American* 268, no. 6 (June 1992): 100–106.

Chandrashekar, J., M.A. Hoon, N.J.P. Ryba, and C.S. Zuker. "The Receptors and Cells for Mammalian Taste." *Nature* 444 (2006): 288–294.

Corcoran A.J., J.R. Barber, and W.E. Conner . W.E. "Tiger Moth Jams Bat Sonar." *Science* 325 (2009): 325–327.

Corkin, S. "What's New with the Amnesic Patient H.M? *Nature Reviews Neuroscience* 3 (2002): 153–160.

Craig, A.D. and Bushnell. M.C. "The Thermal Grill Illusion: Unmasking the Burn of Cold Pain." *Science* 265 (1994): 252–255.

Czeisler, C.A., T.L. Shanahan, E.B. Klerman, H. Martens, D.J. Bortman, J.S Emens, T. Klein, and J.F. Rizzo. "Suppression of Melatonin Secretion in Some Blind Patients by Exposure to Bright Light." *New England Journal of Medicine* 332 (1995): 6–11.

DeWall, C.N., G. MacDonald, G.D. Webster, C.L. Masten, R.F. Baumeister, C. Powell, D. Combs, D.R. Shurtz, T.F. Stillman, D.M. Tice, and N.I. Eisenberger. "Acetaminophen Reduces Social Pain: Behavioral and Neural Evidence." *Psychological Science* 21, no. 7 (2010): 931–937.

DiMaria, S. and Ngai, J. "The Cell Biology of Smell." *The Journal of Cell Biology* 191, no. 3 (2010): 443–452.

Edmund S., and E.S. Higgins. "Do ADHD Drugs Take a Toll on the Brain?" *Scientific American Mind* 20 (Jul 2009): 38–43.

Eisenberger, N.I., M.D. Lieberman, and K.D. Williams. "Does Rejection Hurt? An fMRI Study of Social Exclusion." *Science* 302 (2003): 290–292.

Elbert, T., C. Pantev, C. Wienbruch, B. Rockstroh, and E. Taub. "Increased Cortical Representation of the Fingers of the Left Hand in String Players." *Science* 270, no. 5234 (1995): 305–307.

Ettinger, R.H. *Psychopharmacology*. New York, NY: Prentice Hall, 2010.

Feldman, R., A. Weller, O Zagoory-Sharon, and A. Levine, A. "Evidence for a Neuroendocrinological Foundation of Human Affiliation: Plasma Oxytocin Levels Across Pregnancy and the Postpartum Period Predict Mother-Infant Bonding. *Psychological Science* 18, no. 11 (2007): 965–970.

Fields. R.D. (April 2011). "The Hidden Brain." *Scientific American Mind,* 22 (April 2011): 52–59.

Fleischman, J. *A Gruesome But True Story about Brain Science*. Boston, Mass.: Houghton Mifflin, 2002.

Flier, J.S., and E. Maratos-Flier. "What Fuels Fat." *Scientific American* 297 (September 2007): 72–81.

Formisano, E., D.-S. Kim, F. Di Salle, P.-F. van de Moortele, K. Ugurbil, and R. Goebel. "Mirror-symmetric Tonotopic Maps in Human Primary Auditory Cortex." Neuron 40 (2003): 859–869.

Garstang, M. "Long Distance, Low-frequency Elephant Communication." *Journal of Comparative Physiology: Neuroethology, Sensory, Neural and Behavioral Physiology* 190, no. 10 (2004): 791–805.

Insel, T.R., and L.J. Young. "The Neurobiology of Attachment." *Nature Reviews Neuroscience* 2 (2001): 129–136.

James, W. *Psychology: The Briefer Course.* Mineola, NY: Dover Publishers, 1892 [2001].

Johansson, R.S., and J.R. Flanagan. "Coding and Use of Tactile Signals from the Fingertips in Object Manipulation Tasks." *Nature Reviews Neuroscience* 10 (2009): 345-359.

Julien, R.M., C.D. Advokat, and J. Comaty. *A Primer of Drug Action.* 12th ed. New York, NY: Worth Publishers, 2001.

Klerman, E.B., T.L. Shanahan, D.J. Brotman, D.W. Rimmer, J.S. Emens, J.F. Rizzo, and C.A. Czeisler. "Photic Resetting of the Human Circadian Pacemaker in the Absence of Conscious Vision." *J. Biol. Rhythms* 17 (2002): 548–555.

Kuchinskas, S. *The Chemistry Connection: How the Oxytocin Response Can Help You Find Trust, Intimacy, and Love.* Oakland, Calif.: New Harbinger, 2009.

Lamb, T.D. "Evolution of the Eye." *Scientific American* 305 (June 2011): 64–69.

Lumpkin E.A., and M.J. Caterina. "Mechanisms of Sensory Transduction in the Skin." *Nature* 445, no. 7130 (2007): 858–865.

Lupien, S.J., B.S. McEwen, M.R. Gunnar, and C. Heim. "Effects of Stress Throughout the Lifespan on the Brain, Behavior, and Cognition." *Nature Reviews Neuroscience* 10 (2009): 434– 445.

Martinez-Conde, S., and S.L. Macknik. "Magic and the Brain." *Scientific American* 299 (Dec 2008): 72–79.

Melzack, R. "Phantom Limbs." *Scientific American* 16 (September 2006): 52–59.

Mori, K., H. Nagao, and Y. Yoshihara. "The Olfactory Bulb: Coding and Processing of Odor Molecule Information." *Science* 286 (1999): 711–715.

Nelson, R.J. *An Introduction to Behavioral Endocrinology.* 4th ed. Sunderland, Mass.: Sinauer, 2011.

Nemeroff, C.B. "The Neurobiology of Depression." *Scientific American* 278 (Jun 1998): 42–49.

Petkova V.I., and H.H. Ehrsson. "When Right Feels Left: Referral of Touch and Ownership Between the Hands." *PLoS ONE* 4, no. 9 (2009): e6933.

Pritchard, T.C., D.A. Macaluso, and P.J. Eslinger. "Taste Perception in Patients with Insular Cortex Lesions." *Behavioral Neuroscience* 113, no. 4 (1999): 663–671.

Provencio, I. "The Hidden Organ in Our Eyes." *Scientific American*, 304 (Apr 2011): 54–59.

Ramachandran,V.S., and D. Rogers-Ramachandran, D. "It's All Done with Mirrors." *Scientific American Mind* 18 (August 2007): 16–18.

———. "Phantom Limbs and Neural Plasticity." *Archives of Neurology* 57(2000): 317–320.

Ridding, M.C., and Rothwell, J.C. "Is There a Future for Therapeutic Use of Transcranial Magnetic Stimulation?" *Nature Reviews. Neuroscience,* 8(2007): 559–567.

Ridley, M. *Nature via Nurture. Genes, Experience, and What Makes Us Human.* New York, N.Y: Harper Collins, 2003.

Rosenblum, L.D. *See What I'm Saying. The Extraordinary Powers of Our Five Senses.* New York, N.Y.: W.W. Norton, 2010.

Sacks, O. *An Anthropologist on Mars: Seven Paradoxical Tales.* New York, N.Y.: Knopf, 1995.

———. *The Island of the Colorblind.* New York: N.Y.: Knopf, 1997.

———. *The Man Who Mistook His Wife for a Hat and Other Clinical Tales.* New York N.Y.: Touchstone, 1998.

Saenz, Lewis, L.B., A.G. Huth, I. Fine, and C. Koch. "Visual Motion Area MT+/V5 Responds to Auditory Motion in Human Sight-recovered Subjects." *Journal of Neuroscience* 28, no. 20 (2008): 5141–5148.

Schmelz, M. "Itch and Pain." *Neuroscience and Biobehavioral Reviews* 34, no. 2 (2010): 171–176.

Smith, D.V., and R.F. Margolskee. "Making Sense of Taste." *Scientific American* 16 (September 2006): 84–92.

Thomas, C., T.C. Avidan, G. Humphreys, K. Jung, F. Gao, and M. Behrman. "Reduced Structural Connectivity in Ventral Visual Cortex in Congenital Prosopagnosia." *Nature Neuroscience* 12 (2009): 29–31.

Wenner, M. "A New Kind of Target." *Scientific American* 301 (Aug 2009): 70–76.

Westly, E. "Different Shades of Blue." *Scientific American Mind* 21 (May 2010): 30–37.

Zak, P.J. "The Neurobiology of Trust." *Scientific American* 298 (June 2008): 88–95.

Zaidi, F.H., J.T. Hull, S.N. Pierson, K. Wulff, D. Aeschbach, J.J. Gooley, G.C. Brainard, K. Gregory-Evans, J.F. Rizzo, C.A. Czeisler, et al. "Short-wavelength Light Sensitivity of Circadian, Pupillary and Visual Awareness in Blind Humans Lacking a Functional Outer Retina." *Current Biology* 17 (2007): 2122–2128.

Zeki, S. "Cerebral Akinetopsia (Visual Motion Blindness). *Brain* 114 (1991): 811–824.

Zihl, J. d. vonCramon, and N. Mai. "Selective Disturbance of Movement Vision After Bilateral Brain Damage." *Brain* 106 (1983): 313–340.

INDEX

Note: Page numbers followed by *g* indicate glossary entries.

A

accessory visual cortices 88, 89–93
acetylcholine (ACh) 113*g*
   agonists of 105
   metabolism of 105
   as neurotransmitter 100, 105
acetylcholinesterase (AChE) 105
acetylcholinesterase inhibitors 105, 110
ACh. *See* acetylcholine
AChE. *See* acetylcholinesterase
achromatopsia 90–91
ACTH (adrenocorticotropic hormone) 38
action potential 27, 28–31, 99–100
   in myelinated v. unmyelinated axon 31
   toxins and 30–31
ADHD (attention deficit hyperactivity disorder) 106–107, 110
adoption studies 18, 20
adrenal gland 36
adrenal hormones 35–38
adrenocorticotropic hormone (ACTH) 38
ageusia 58, 113*g*
agnosia, movement 3
agonists, drug 105–108, 110
AIDS/HIV 27
A. J. (hyperthymesia study) 2
akinetopsia 3, 93, 94–95, 113*g*
alcoholism, evoked potentials in 9
alexia 2

alien limb syndrome 3
all-or-none action potential 99
ALS (amyotrophic lateral sclerosis) 27, 113*g*
Alzheimer's disease 27, 105, 110
amacrine cells 81
amino acid neurotransmitters 99, 100, 113*g*
amnesia, anterograde 2
amphetamine(s) 103
amphetamine-induced psychosis 103, 113*g*
amplitude 73–74, 79
amputation, phantom limb after 3, 70, 117*g*
amusia 3
amyotrophic lateral sclerosis (ALS) 27, 113*g*
androsterone, odor of 57
animal studies 13–14
   color vision 82
   echolocation 75
   genetic 21–22
   hormones 40–42
anosmia 56–57, 113*g*
antagonists, drug 105–108, 110
anterograde amnesia 2
Anthropologist on Mars, An (Sacks) 91
antibiotics, ototoxicity of 79
antidepressants 105, 109, 110
antipsychotic drugs 103, 108, 110
anxiety
   genetics of 17–18
   psychoactive drugs for 109, 110
aphasia, Broca's 4–6, 12